Revelation and The Great Controversy

By
George E. Rice

TEACH Services, Inc.
www.TEACHServices.com

_____

Copyright © 2009 George Rice and TEACH Services, Inc.
ISBN-13: 978-1-57258-606-2 (Paperback)
ISBN-13: 978-1-57258-984-1 (Ebook)
Library of Congress Control Number: 2009933833

Published by
TEACH Services, Inc.
www.TEACHServices.com

Contents

Chapter One

What This Book Is About

I was just entering high school when I enrolled in the *20ᵗʰ Century Bible Correspondence Course*. I knew a little about the Seventh-day Adventist Church because my grandfather had been a Seventh-day Adventist. However, he asked to have his name dropped from the church records when America entered World War II. He was a supervisor at a munitions factory and felt obligated to work on the Sabbath in defense of his country. I had been to church two or three times as a child, but my parents did not take religion very seriously. As I got into the Bible lessons I began doing some serious thinking, at least it was serious for a teenager. Could the prophecies of Daniel and Revelation really be understood?

By this time the war was over, my grandparents and other members of the family were living with us on a small farm in Connecticut. One day while looking for something in the attic of our old New England farm house, I came across a box of books. Upon opening it I recognized several of the books that my grandfather had on some of his bookshelves years ago. I remembered looking through them as a child because I was fascinated with the pictures in them. They were colporteur editions of the Conflict of the Ages Series by Ellen G. White. I took two of them to my bedroom and began reading *The Desire of*

Ages and *The Great Controversy*. It was *The Great Controversy* that helped me to develop some understanding of the apocalyptic prophecies in Scripture. Although my understanding was very limited at the time, over the years these prophecies have become clearer and clearer. Looking back at these early years, I realize how much I am indebted to the old *20ᵗʰ Century Bible Course* and my grandfather's collection of the Conflict of the Ages series.

By the way, my whole family was eventually baptized and became Seventh-day Adventists. Grandfather was rebaptized and joined the rest of us.

As a pastor and teacher, since those early years, I have had a deep interest in the Book of Revelation. I also realize the crucial role this prophetic book is playing in alerting God's people to the times in which we now live, in preparing them for the final conflict, and in strengthening their commitment to stand firm for truth when lies and deceptions will threaten to engulf them.

I have found that few long-time members of God's remnant church really understand what Revelation presents and that newly baptized members are completely overwhelmed by Revelation's prophecies and symbols, much as I was as a teenager. Although both groups are kept in mind as this little book is written, it is prepared especially for the second group. It is my desire to make the prophecies of Revelation meaningful for babes in the faith. Something which I wish I had as I made my way through the *20ᵗʰ Century Bible Course*.

Here is what this study is about. *Revelation For Beginners* is to help people who are just beginning to study the only prophetic book in the New Testament. Its purpose is to give a general overview of the book's prophecies and content. The approach taken to achieve this goal is to look at Revelation's thematic structure. The overall theme of this prophetic book is the great controversy between Christ and

Satan. The thematic structure as presented in its prophecies helps us to understand the nature of this controversy, how it will be fought, and its outcome.

Do not expect to find a detailed exposition of prophecy. *Revelation For Beginners* is not a commentary. However, certain sections of Revelation will be looked at in some detail while others will be simply mentioned so you can follow the thematic flow from prophecy to prophecy. What is important for you, as the student of Revelation, is to see how the great controversy between Christ and Satan is played out and finally resolved in these prophecies.

The Author

The importance of the Book of Revelation cannot be over stated as we move into the final events of the great controversy. Its prophecies lay out the course that the church of Christ would follow down through the Christian ages and the experiences that are in store for her as the great controversy reaches its climax. The prophecies in the last half of this book are of utmost importance for us today. Because of the nature of the great controversy and the events involved in the destiny of God's people, the writer of these prophecies was carefully chosen.

To help those who have not read Revelation much because they have felt its prophecies are too difficult to understand or those who are just beginning to read the Bible for the first time, we will take a few minutes to get acquainted with its author. The author of Revelation simply refers to himself as John, the servant of Jesus (Rev. 1:1). John was so well known in the early church at the time this book was written it was not necessary for him to say anything more about himself other than give his name. He was the youngest among the twelve apostles. He and his older brother, the apostle James, were originally fishermen and business partners with the apostles Peter and Andrew

(Lk. 5:8-10). James and John prospered under the management of their father Zebedee, which is evident from the fact that Zebedee had hired help (Mark 1:19, 20). But John, with his brother James, left the thriving family business and became disciples of the Teacher who had nothing of this world's goods and nowhere to lay His head.

Jesus called James and John "Sons of Thunder" (Mk. 3:17), which gives a clue as to their personalities when they first joined Jesus' team. But under the grace and patience of Jesus, John changed, as, no doubt, did his brother. *"In the life of the disciple John true sanctification is exemplified. . . . Day by day his heart was drawn out to Christ, until he lost sight of self in love for his Master."*[1] Of all of the apostles, John entered into the deepest spiritual relationship with Jesus. He felt the deepest empathy for Him. The relationship between the Savior and John was so deep and vibrant, John could refer to himself as *"the disciple whom Jesus loved"* (John 13:23; 21:20).

Knowing who Jesus really is and feeling the power of His saving love was an experience that John never forgot. His heart thrilled every time the thought entered his mind that he had seen God and he had touched Him. John tries to convey his feelings in the opening statement of his first epistle, *"That which was from the beginning, which we have heard, which we have seen with our eyes, which we have looked upon, and our hands have handled, concerning the Word of life—the life was manifested, and we have seen, and bear witness and declare to you that eternal life which was with the Father and was manifested to us."* (1 John:1, 2)

You and I will not be able to share in John's experience until we are in the kingdom with Jesus. Knowing this, John encourages us by sharing what is available to us now, *i.e.*, a vibrant spiritual fellowship with our Lord. For he goes on to say, *"That which we have seen and heard we declare to you, that you also may have fellowship with us;*

and truly our fellowship is with the Father and with His Son Jesus Christ" (1 John 1:3).

On the basis of Ellen White's description of the relationship each apostle had with Jesus, we can construct the following pyramid with John being the closest to Him:

John

Peter and James

Matthew, Andrew, Philip, Nathanael

Thomas, James of Alphaeus, Simon the Zealot, Judas of James

Judas Iscariot

Ellen White says that Jesus loved them all, but it was John that found the deepest and richest relationship with the Savior.[2] It was this disciple who was entrusted with the visions recorded in Revelation. In addition to Revelation, John wrote one of the four gospels and three epistles, I, II, and III John.

Prophetic Model of Inspiration

Another thing that is important for those who are just beginning to read Revelation is to be aware of the fact that John outlines step-by-step how the visions of the book were transmitted to him. Luke, who wrote the gospel that bears his name, is the only other Bible writer who gives us details as to how he received the information that is recorded in his book. John's explanation of his source of information can be called the prophetic model of inspiration. Luke's explanation of his sources can be called the research model. Luke did not have visions as John did when he wrote Revelation. Luke collected information for his gospel by interviewing eye witnesses and those who were ministers of the word (Lk. 1:1-4). The other biblical books contain no *detailed* information as to the process of inspiration that led to their writing. Some of the of the Old Testament prophets simply say, "The Lord said," or The word of the Lord came to me," or "I saw." There is no step-by-step detail as we read in the opening verses of Revelation.

As John begins to write out the visions contained in Revelation, he clearly outlines the successive steps by which they came to him (Rev. 1:1, 2). These steps are as follows: 1) God the Father gave to Jesus the revelation of what was to shortly come to past. 2) Jesus sent the revelation to his servant John. 3) The authenticity of this revelation was confirmed by the attending angel, no doubt it was Gabriel. 4) John, in turn, sent the revelation to the seven churches in the Roman province of Asia (modern Turkey).

Although the Holy Spirit is not mentioned in these successive steps, we know that He had an active role in the writing of this prophetic book. For Jesus had told His disciples that the Holy Spirit would be the One who would show them things to come (John 16:13). It was the work of the Spirit to convey the revelations from Jesus to John and then assist him in writing them out. John acknowledges the role of the Spirit in receiving his visions when he says, "*I was in the Spirit on the Lord's Day*" (Rev. 1:10) and "*So he carried me away in the Spirit*" (Rev. 17:3).

Perhaps it would be well to clear up a misunderstanding at this point. The first words of this book are, "*The Revelation of Jesus Christ.*" It has been assumed that this phrase means that the content of this book is a revelation about Jesus—who He is, etc. While it is true that Revelation tells us much about Jesus, that is not what this phase is saying. It is telling us that the content of the book is a revelation from God the Father that was passed on to Jesus and He sent it to John (following the steps in the model given above). To all intent and purposes, Jesus is the Originator, the Source, of Revelation's prophecies. The content of the book is an account of what "*must shortly take place*" (Rev. 1:1).

Method of Interpretation

Another point that will help the reader of *Revelation For Beginners* is to understand the method of interpreting prophecy that is used in this book. As we move from prophecy to prophecy, we will follow the historical method of interpretation. There are three major methods of interpreting the prophecies found in Revelation. One method sees all the prophecies as already fulfilled. This is called preterism. The second sees only a few having been fulfilled with the majority of the prophecies to be fulfilled in the future. This is called futurism. The third method of interpretation sees some of the prophecies as already fulfilled, some are presently being fulfilled, and some are yet to be fulfilled. This is called historicism. Seventh-day Adventists have traditionally followed the historical method of interpreting prophecy and this is the approach adopted in this book.

Chiastic Structure

Now a statement on Revelation's structure. Kenneth A. Strand[3] and C. Mervyn Maxwell[4] have demonstrated that the prophecies in Revelation are presented in chiastic structure. A chiasm is a series of parallels much like a two-sided stepladder. The bottom two steps are parallel to each other. The second two steps are parallel, etc., on up the stepladder. An example of a simple chiasm that exists in one verse can be found in Acts 2:42, "*And they continued steadfastly in the apostles' doctrine and fellowship, in the breaking of bread, and in prayer.*" The structure is as follows:

a. Apostles' doctrine (teaching)

  b. Fellowship

  b.′ Breaking bread

a.′ Prayer

Apostles' doctrine (a) is parallel to prayer (a') and fellowship (b) is parallel to breaking bread (b'). A and a' are the spiritual activities of the early church while b and b'are the social activities of the church.

The work of Strand and Maxwell has made a valuable contribution to the understanding of Revelation's prophecies. For the beginner, however, working with the chiastic structure of Revelation may be a bit overwhelming. It might be easier to work with the thematic flow of the prophecies which in no way upsets or contradicts Revelation's chiastic structure. An understanding of the thematic structure of this book may prove to be the starting point for the beginner that will lead to its deeper study in the future.

Thematic Structure

As stated above, the great controversy between Christ and Satan is the theme of Revelation. Its prophecies show how this controversy will be fought by revealing the military strategies on both sides of the conflict. Rev. 12 is the thematic center of the book, and around this center all of its prophecies revolve. This chapter introduces the great controversy and divides the conflict between good and evil into four major battles. Although only four battles are presented in this chapter they are models of how countless millions are fought day-by-day, year-by-year, and century-by-century. The first battle covers the ages of time during which rebellion appeared and ripened in heaven (12:7-12). The second, third, and fourth battles present the conflict as it was to be fought during the centuries of Christian history. Battle two presents Satan's attempt to stop the plan of redemption by destroying Christ during His life on earth (12:1-5). Battle three reveals Satan attempt to destroy Jesus' followers from the time of His ascension to the end of the 1,260 prophetic years (12:6,13-16). Battle four is Satan's war on the remnant people of God (12:17).

When John received the visions that are recorded in Revelation, battles one and two were history, battle three was just beginning, and battle four was yet future. From our point in time, battles one, two, and three are past and we are now in battle four. This is why Revelation is so important to you and me today, and why Satan does not want people to study and understand it. The thematic structure of Revelation can be illustrated by the following diagram:

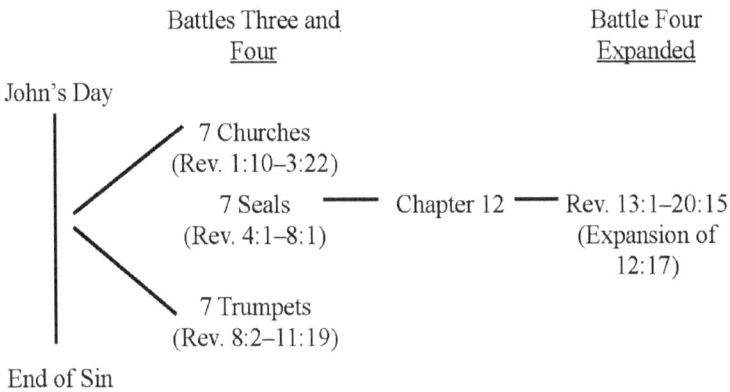

```
                    Battles Three and              Battle Four
                         Four                        Expanded
   John's Day
      |           ╱  7 Churches
      |          ╱   (Rev. 1:10–3:22)
      |         ╱
      |        ╱        7 Seals   ——  Chapter 12  ——  Rev. 13:1–20:15
      |        ╲        (Rev. 4:1–8:1)                (Expansion of
      |         ╲                                        12:17)
      |          ╲
      |           ╲  7 Trumpets
      |              (Rev. 8:2–11:19)
   End of Sin
```

The prophecies listed under battles three and four give an overview of Satan's war against Jesus' followers and cover the periods of church history from John's day to the end of the controversy. According to Rev. 12:17, Satan will war against God's remnant people in battle four. Rev. 13:1-20:15 reveal how battle four will be fought. In other words, Rev. 13:1-20:15 is an expansion and explanation of Rev.12:17.

The three prophecies in battles three and four function similar to Dan. 2, 7, and 8. They are recapitulations, that is to say, they cover the same period of history but each prophecy introduces details that the other two do not have.

Our purpose now is to spend some time with Chapter 12 and then

9

follow the thematic flow of the prophecies that revolve around it. This experience should give you a foundation upon which to build as you journey deeper into the exciting prophecies of Revelation.

References

1. White, Ellen G. *The Acts of the Apostles*, Mountain View, CA, Pacific Press Publishing Association, (1911), p. 557.

2. _____, *The Desire of Ages*, Boise, ID, Pacific Press Publishing Association, (1940), p. 292.

3. Strand, Kenneth A. "The Eight Basic Visions" and "Victorious—Introduction Scenes," *Symposium on Revelation-Book I*, Frank B. Holbrook (ed.), Silver Spring, Biblical Research Institute, (1992), pp. 35-72.

4. Maxwell, C. Mervyn, *God Cares*, vol. 2, Nampa, ID, Pacific Press Publishing Association, (1985), pp. 54-62.

Chapter Two

The Great Controversy

When I became a Seventh-day Adventist, I was convinced that the Lord would come back to get His people within at least five years. You have to remember, I was a teenager in the first years of high school. This conviction was deepened during the first camp-meeting I attended in South Lancaster, MA. My mother sent me off to campmeeting with my uncle and aunt. The plan was that I would attend the first weekend and return with my uncle on Sunday night because he had to be at work Monday morning. My aunt had a family tent reserved so she could stay the whole week.

When it came time for my uncle to return home, I made up my mind that I wanted to stay. I did not have enough clothes for the week and my mother thought I should come home. But my aunt assured my mother that we could work things out and I was allowed to stay. I attended most of the adult meetings, and they had a profound impact on my life. I returned home with an even deeper conviction that Jesus would come to get His people soon. He had to come back before the next five years were over. But He hasn't come back yet and many five year periods have passed. But the delay has not lessened the conviction that the end of all things is upon us and Jesus will be here soon. Revelation is most helpful in opening our understanding as to where we are in the flow of human history.

As the beginner picks up the Bible and turns to the Book of Revelation, it is important to understand that human history is approaching its climax, therefore the prophecies of Revelation are to occupy more and more of his time, study, and thought, especially those contained in chapters thirteen through twenty. These prophecies lay out for us the course of the war against God's remnant and unfold the strategy and maneuvering of the enemy. They are accurate intelligence reports of what is to happen in the future and upon which our eternal life depends. This is why Revelation is so important to the remnant.

Speaking of this importance, Ellen White said, "The solemn messages that have been given in their order in the Revelation are to occupy the first place in the minds of God's people."[1] And the reason these prophecies are to occupy the first place in our thinking is to protect us from the final deceptions. "The Savior foretold that in the latter days false prophets would appear, and draw away disciples after them; and also that those who in this time of peril should stand faithful to the truth that is specified in the book of Revelation would have to meet doctrinal errors so specious that, if it were possible, the very elect would be deceived."[2]

As we have already noted, Chapter 12 introduces the conflict between good and evil. Not only is this chapter the foundation of the prophecies in Revelation, it is the basis for understanding biblical history. In fact, understanding Chapter 12 is very helpful in coming to grips with what is going on in your own life. When you read Chapter 12, you are at the core of the sin problem, at the center of the battles in your own life which you know all too well. Therefore it is here where we must begin.

Battle One

The first two battles in Rev. 12 are not in chronological order. Battle one is presented in verses 7-12 and introduces us to the origin of the great controversy. These verses present the following insights: 1) war broke out in heaven, 2) Michael and His angels fought against the dragon (Satan) and his angels, 3) Satan and his angels were exiled to planet earth, 4) humans who are loyal to Jesus overcome Satan by the blood of the Lamb, their living testimony, and not loving their lives to the death, and 5) Satan came to Planet Earth with great wrath because he knows his time is short. These five points which give us an insight into battle one deserve some investigation.

1. The first question that must be resolved concerns the nature of the war in heaven. When we talk of war today, we pull up mental pictures of bloodshed and death. However, until Adam and Eve sinned, death was unknown in the universe. Since battle one precedes Adam's fall, this battle was not one of fisticuffs and firefights. It was a war of ideas, error challenging truth, it was an ideological war. When Satan and his angels were expelled from heaven and placed on earth, they brought this tactic of warfare with them. It can be seen in the garden of Eden as Satan tempted Eve, *"Has God indeed said, 'You shall not eat of every tree of the garden?'...God knows that in the day you eat of it your eyes will be opened, and you will be like God, knowing good and evil."* (Gen. 3:1, NKJV). Eve was faced with the question as to who she should believe, God or Satan. Should she accept God's word as truth, or Satan's? Unfortunately she believed Satan and convinced Adam to follow her. So the great controversy entered human history by means of an ideological tactic. We will see how the ideological phase of the conflict between truth and error

works itself out in battles three and four. Physical persecution and death entered the great controversy after Adam's sin.

2. Michael led the loyal angels in this conflict with Satan. Many believe that Michael is an exalted angel or the first angel among the heavenly host. However, the Scriptures present Jesus as Michael. Here is the evidence for this: 1) the Hebrew name Michael means "Who is like God?" The implications of this name do not fit an angel, for they are created creatures. Only One who is divine and Self-existing can be identified by the question raised in the name "Michael." 2) In Dan. 12:1, Michael is called the Prince of Daniel's people. A prince is a member of a royal family and heir to the throne. At His incarnation, Jesus joined the human race; human yet divine, the second Person of the Godhead, Heir to the heavenly throne, and Prince of His people. An angel would not fit into this category for an angel is not a member of the Royal Family thus he cannot be an heir to the throne, the Prince of Daniel's people. No angel has become incarnate in human flesh and has joined the human race. Only Jesus fits this description. 3) In Jude 9 Michael is called the archangel.

The Greek word for archangel is αρχαγγελος, which is made up of two words, αρχη meaning "beginning" and αγγελος meaning "messenger" or "angel." Αρχη or "beginning" in Greek can have an active or a passive meaning, just as "beginning" does in English. Using an illustration in English, we can say that "Adam was the beginning of the human race" (passive), but we can also say that "Adam was the beginning of the human race" (active). The passive use of the word means that Adam was the product of creation, he had nothing to do with his origin or beginning, and was the first of his kind to exist. The active use of the word means that Adam fathered the human race and is the ancestor of us all, thus the beginning of the human race. Since Jesus is the Creator of all life in the universe (Col. 1:16), and He is called Michael because He is like God, and He is the Royal Prince, "Archangel" must be understood in its active form. Michael (Jesus) is the Originator or Creator of the angels.

3. When Satan was expelled from heaven, the angels who chose him as their leader were expelled with him. By the time of the expulsion, Satan had become the leader of an opposition party. The prophet Isaiah clearly states his ambitions, *"I will ascend into heaven, I will exalt my throne above the stars of God....I will be like the Most High"* (14:13, 14). Speaking of Satan's ambitions, Ellen White says, *"And coveting the honor which the infinite Father had bestowed upon His Son, this prince of angels aspired to power which it was the prerogative of Christ alone to wield."*[3] Anyone who covets the prerogative of Christ and to be worship as Christ deserves to be worshiped is an antichrist. Satan is the original antichrist.

The Greek word αντιχριστος ("antichrist") is made up of a preposition, αντι which takes the ablitive case of exchange, and χριστος which is the word translated Christ. We generally think of "anti" as meaning to be against someone or something. But this is a derivative idea growing out of desiring to take someone else's place. If a person works to usurp another person, he is indeed against that person. An antichrist wants to take the place of Christ and receive to himself the worship and honor that is due Christ. Satan uses human antichrists to divert to himself the worship that is due Christ. He stands behind these visible "fronts" to deflect to himself the honor, worship, and obedience that is due to Christ alone. As John wrote his first epistle, he told his readers that already there were many antichrists in the world (1 John 2:18). There were, for example, all of the Greek and Roman gods and goddesses in the pagan pantheons of John's day that were being worshiped. Then there was, of course, the Roman emperor who demanded worship as a god from his subjects. They all served as a front for Satan. Today, we have millions of pagan gods who are worshiped throughout the world. Then there is the antichrist within Christianity.

The angels that chose to go with Satan have become his demons. The spirit priest that was preparing Roger Morneau for indoctrination into a satanic cult, divided these demons into three groups. In the following quotes from Morneau's book, *A Trip Into The Supernatural*, the spirit priest identified the three groups as follows:

1. *"He defined the friendly spirits as those of great intellect who have ability to impersonate the dead."*

2. *"'The warriors,' he said, 'concentrated on sowing discord in families and misunderstanding between friends, relatives, and neighbors. Such spirits love to create friction between races and other segments of society. And those who have the best track record in dividing people and filling them with hatred and violence, Satan assigns the task of causing out-right war among nations.'"*

3. *"'The oppressors,' the spiritist leader explained, 'are a unique group in that they find delight only in producing misery and destruction among the human race. They suffered some kind of mental breakdown when our great master and his spirit associates were misunderstood and driven to this planet, and they have never recovered from the ordeal. Hating the Creator bitterly, they feel that the only way to get even with Him is to wreck the lives of those created in His image.'"*[4]

There are many today who believe that Satan and his demons exist only in mythology. But battle one of Rev. 12 makes it clear that their existence is no myth and that their anger is very real.

4. Although the forces of evil are strong, Jesus gave to John a glimpse of the future so he and his readers would not be overwhelmed by what was introduced by battle one. Victory over Satan and his demons belongs to those who have accepted the blood of the Lamb for the forgiveness of their sins and who bear witness to His love. It is Satan's goal in the great controversy to break the will of God's people and separate them from their Source of strength. But victory will not be denied them. *"They did not love their lives to the death"* (12:11).

5. As battle one comes to its conclusion, Satan is pictured as being filled with great anger. He is isolated to earth with his angels and he knows his time is short. He has been on earth for some 6,000 years now, how can this be a short period of time? We do not know how long Lucifer has lived. It could be many millions of years, or possibly longer. In comparison to the period of time he has already lived, his sojourn on earth is short. The fact that he has only a short period of time suggests that his life will soon end.

Having introduced the great controversy in battle one, John is now led by inspiration through battles two, three, and four.

Battle Two

Rev.12 jumps over the Old Testament history of the great controversy by moving directly from Satan's expulsion from heaven at the end of battle one to the birth of Jesus. The incarnate Son of God is the object of battle two (12:1-5). This battle begins with the prophetic imagery of a beautiful, virtuous woman clothed with the sun who is about to give birth to a male Child. The dragon, which is the prophetic representation of Satan, stands before the woman ready to pounce upon the Child when He is born. However, the Child is snatched up to the throne of God and He will rule all nations with a rod of iron.

A woman in prophecy represents God's people. God's Old Testament people are called "the daughter of Zion" (Isa. 1:8; 10:32; 37:32), God declares Himself to be the Husband of His people (Isa.54:5), and He looks upon His people as His wife saying He is married to them (Jer. 4:14), unfaithfulness to God is looked upon as breaking the marriage relationship and as spiritual adultery (Jer. 3:8). The woman in battle two represents God's faithful people through whom the Messiah would come into the world. This same woman who gave birth to the Messiah is the woman who Satan tries to destroy after the ascension of Jesus. Therefore, she stands as a prophetic type of God's people through all the ages of human history.

Why is battle two introduced before battle one? Why are these two battles not in chronological order? Battle two was Satan's attempt to destroy Christ while He was here on earth and thus thwart the plan of salvation. He is pictured in Revelation as poised to pounce upon the Child as soon as He is born.

It is battle two that won the war of the great controversy, although other battles were to follow. The importance of battle two can be illustrated by an engagement between the United States and Japan during World War II. The battle of Midway in the Pacific won the war for the United States. In this engagement, the back of the Japanese navy and its naval air force was broken. Many battles followed Midway before World War II was over. But this test of naval and air strength turn the tide in favor of the United States.

So it was in the great controversy. If Satan had been successful in his attacks and Christ had failed, the great controversy would have been decided in Satan's favor. But Christ was victorious, He arose in a glorious resurrection. The back of Satan's rebellion was broken and the war was won. The four gospels contain the record of battle two. In Revelation 12, Midway in the great controversy is presented first to give its readers assurance that Satan is a defeated enemy, then in this context the three other battles are presented.

Let's pause here to look at an interesting point that is brought out in the Greek text. It is the use of the word "crown." The woman wore a crown of twelve stars (Rev. 12:1). The Greek word here is στεφανος, a garland (NKJV) or a chaplet made of vegetation. The woman's στεφανος, however, is made of jewels. This type of crown made of various types of vegetation is a symbol of victory. They were the "gold medals" in the ancient Greek Olympic games. Paul speaks of the crown that the victor receives only to have it fade away in a few days (1 Cor. 9:25). The crown of thorns placed upon Jesus' head was a στεφανος (Mt. 27:29). It was made and placed upon His head in an act of mockery and defiance. But this crown became the symbol of victory over sin and Satan.

The red dragon in battle two has seven heads and crowns on each of them. The crowns that the dragon wears are diadems (NKJV) from the Greek word διαδημα which is a blue ribbon with white embroidery. The blue ribbon was a symbol of political power. The NKJV makes the distinction between the two crowns by calling one a garland (symbol of victory) and the other a diadem (symbol of political power). In Rev.19, Jesus is pictured as a Warrior-King leading the armies of heaven against the coalition of evil that is bent upon the destruction of His people. As a Warrior-King He is pictured as wearing many crowns (διαδηματα, blue ribbons) because He is King of kings and Lord of lords (19:12, 16).

Having lost the war by failing in battle two, Satan turns in anger upon the followers of Jesus who are still represented by the woman in battle three and upon her remnant in battle four.

Battle Three

When John received the visions which make up the Book of Revelation, battles one and two were over and battle three had already begun. Therefore the prophecies of Revelation address the warfare in battles three and four. Satan had failed to stop the plan of redemption in battle two. Jesus had risen from the dead, ascended to His position at the Father's right hand, and was directing the conflict against Satan on earth.

As we pick up John's account of battle three (Rev. 12:6, 13-16), we must be aware of the parenthesis that separates the introduction to this battle (v. 6) from the remainder of its description (vv. 13-16). The account begins with the woman (Jesus' followers) fleeing into the wilderness after Jesus' ascension where God watches over her (v 6). At this point the description of battle three is interrupted by the introduction of battle one (vv. 7-12). John then picks up battle three (vv. 13-16) describing Satan's attempt to sweep away the woman with a flood of water out of his mouth, and the earth opening up its mouth and swallowing the flood. In these few verses we have a summary of the conflict between truth and error from the early history of the Christian church, down through the middle ages, to the opening up of the new world which became a haven of refuge for those who wanted to flee religious intolerance and persecution.

The flood of water introduced in battle three represents the attacks launched by the Church of Rome against those who opposed her teaching and who were considered heretics. After a detailed description of these attacks in earlier volumes, Philip Schaff gives a quick summary of Rome's attempt to silence descent as he begins volume seven and the Protestant reformation in Germany:

"The persecution of heretics reached its height in the papal crusades against the Albigenses under Innocent III., one of the best of popes; in the dark deeds of the Spanish Inquisition; and in the unspeakable atrocities of the Duke of Alva against the Protestants in the Netherlands during his short reign (1567-1573).

"The most cruel of the many persecutions of the innocent Waldenses in the valleys of Piedmont took place in 1655, and shocked by its boundless violence the whole Protestant world, calling forth the vigorous protest of Cromwell and inspiring the famous sonnet of Milton, his foreign secretary:

> *"Avenge, O Lord, thy slaughtered saints, whose bones*
> *Lie scattered on the Alpine mountains cold,*
> *Even them who kept thy truth so pure of old,*
> *When all our fathers worshiped stocks and stones."*[5]

Within the context of John's description of battle three, the 1,260 year prophecy is mentioned twice (vv. 6, 14). Thus impressing upon our minds the importance of locating this time prophecy within its proper place as the great controversy unfolds. This helps us to place the little horn of Dan. 7 (*cf.*, v 25) and the sea beast of Rev. 13 (*cf.*, v. 5) in their historical context. For both the little horn and the sea beast are given power to do their work for 1,260 years, the period of time that is anchored in the third battle.

Again, it is important to understand that the woman of Rev. 12:1-5 (God's Old Testament church) who gave birth to the male Child is the same woman that Satan tries to destroy in battle three (God's New Testament church). In Revelation, there is no segregation between old and new. God's church moves on from century to century as a unified people until Jesus returns.

Battle Four

Battle four is presented in the last verse of this chapter (12:17). Satan is described as being enraged with the woman and launching his final campaign upon the remnant of God's people. This remnant is identified by two characteristics, they *"keep the commandments of God and have the testimony of Jesus Christ."* The fact that the remnant are identified by these two characteristics underlines the fact that God's people throughout history are not divided into two groups, old and new. For all of His people, no matter when they have lived, are 1) obedient to Him, and 2) have been given the gift of prophecy. The gift by which God communicates with His faithful people.

Satan hates the remnant. They are living testimony that he does not own and control Planet Earth. They defy his claims by worshiping and honoring God in observing the memorial of His creative power and His ownership of earth. They keep the seventh-day Sabbath which was blessed and sanctified at creation as a sign of their allegiance to their Creator.

Because of this hatred, God prepares His remnant for what lies ahead by expanding battle four which is introduced in Rev. 12:17 by means of the prophecies found in Rev. 13:1 to 20:15. These chapters tell us how Satan will wage war on the remnant and how God responds to this military offensive against His people. We will now return to the beginning of the Book of Revelation and see how the prophecies preceding Chapter 12 fit into battles three and four.

References

1. White, Ellen G. *Testimonies For The Church*, vol. 8, Mountain View, CA, Pacific Press Publishing Association, (1928), p. 302.

2. _____, *Manuscript 11*, 1906.

3. _____, *The Great Controversy,* Boise, ID, Pacific Press Publishing Association, (1911), p. 494

4. Morneau, Roger J. *A Trip Into The Supernatural*, Hagerstown, MD, Review and Herald Publishing Association, (1993), pp. 63, 64.

5. Schaff, Philip, *History of the Christian Church*, (vol. 7), Peabody, MA, Hendrickson Publishers, (Originally published 1888, second printing, 2002), pp. 56, 57.

Chapter Three

Churches, Seals And Trumpets

Now that the thematic structure of Revelation has been introduced and the significance and role of Chapter 12 has been established, we are ready to look at each prophecy and examine its contribution to the overall theme of the great controversy. Revelation opens with three prophecies (Chapters 1 to 11). Each prophecy individually covers the history of the Christian church to the conclusion of the great controversy. Although these prophecies encompass battles three and four, the largest portion of their content is set within battle three. Because they extend to the conclusion of the great controversy, the finale of each prophecy is part of battle four. For example, in the prophecy of the seven churches, Laodicea is set in the context of battle four, as are the sixth and seventh seals and the seventh trumpet. Battle four, as we have seen earlier, is expanded with much more detail in Rev. 13:1-20:15.

The purpose of the recapitulation in the prophecies of the churches, seals, and trumpets is to give more detail on major events in the great controversy. This same approach, as we noted earlier, can be seen in the three prophecies of Dan. 2, 7, 8. It must also be noted that each of these three prophecies in Revelation begins with an introductory scene and then moves to the content of the prophecy.

As the prophecies of the churches, seals, and trumpets are studied, it is helpful to keep in mind that there are two military tactics used in the war between Christ and Satan. First there is the clash between truth and error, or the ideological tactic. Then there is the physical conflict, persecution, or the firefights. These two military tactic are evident in the prophecies of the churches, seals, and trumpets. If this basic understanding is kept in mind, the meaning of these three prophecies will become clear.

Seven Churches

The introductory scene to the prophecy of the seven churches is a vision of Jesus (Rev. 1:9-20). He appears to John on the Isle of Patmos and commissions John to write out the visions he was about to receive and to send them to the seven churches in the Roman province of Asia (modern-day Turkey, Rev. 1:9-20). With the limitations of human language, John tries to describe the glory and majesty of Jesus' appearance. He was clothed with a garment that extended to His feet and He had a golden band around His waist. His hair was as white as snow, His eyes were like flashing fire, His feet looked like polished brass, His voice sounded like the roaring surf of many waters, and His face radiated the glory of the sun shining in all of its strength (Rev. 1:13-16). Following his verbal description of Jesus' appearance and Jesus' explanation of the seven lamp stands and the seven stars in His right hand (Rev. 1:20), John records the first prophecy in Revelation.

You will remember that the great controversy began as an ideological war in heaven. This military tactic of lies and errors has been used by Satan throughout the history of the human race. In the study of the messages to the seven churches, it is important to recognize that these messages open up for us the ideological phase of the great controversy down through the Christian centuries. Through cunning lies and outright error, Satan would lead the professed followers of Jesus farther and farther away from biblical truth. Error would be clothed in sacramental robes.

Paul warned the early Christians that this would happen. To the spiritual leaders in the church at Ephesus, Paul said, *"For I know this, that after my departure savage wolves will come in among you, not sparing the flock. Also from among yourselves men will rise up, speaking perverse things, to draw away the disciples after themselves"* (Acts 20:29, 30). Paul also warned the Thessalonian Christians about the mystery of lawlessness that would enter the church and the lawless one who would appear and work all kinds of deceptions (2 Thess. 2:7-12).

The messages to the seven churches accurately record the actual historical experiences of these churches in Asia Minor. These historical spiritual experiences represent what would happen within the spiritual experience of the Christian church as it moved through seven phases of church history. The messages to the churches (Rev. 2, 3) briefly outline the progressive apostasy of the Christian church and the issues involved in this ideological war. While the experiences of these seven churches represent, primarily, seven phases in the history of the church, they also present experiences that individual congregations are going through today as well as experiences of individual Christians themselves.

The church at Ephesus (Rev. 2:1-7), the first of the seven churches, is commended for many virtues, but this church has begun to lose its first love for Jesus. Here is represented the beginning of the church's fall from spiritual purity. However, the Christians represented by Ephesus are commended for their rejection of the behavior and teaching of the Nicolaitans (Rev. 2:6). The Nicolatians introduced and held to an early heresy that reflected the main issue in the ideological con-

27

flict that was the foundation for the first battle in heaven. They refused to be bound by the requirements of God's law. The Ephesians hated this teaching and so does Jesus (Rev. 2:6).

The message to the second church, Smyrna (Rev. 2:8-11), reveals the suffering of those who resisted the attacks from paganism, the government sponsored religion of the day, and the encroachment of error into the church. But when we get to the third church, Pergamus (Rev. 2:12-17), apostasy from biblical truth becomes clearly apparent. First, the Christians of this period in church history were embracing the deeds and teaching of the Nicolatians even though Jesus emphasizes again that He hates this doctrine (Rev. 2:15). And, in addition to this, the doctrine of Balaam was prevalent in the church.

From the Old Testament story of Balaam (Num. 22-24) and his plot to bring the wrath of God down upon Israel (Num. 31:16), it is clear that the doctrine of Balaam is one of compromise. Concerning Balaam's scheme to destroy Israel, Ellen White says, *"If they [Israel] could be led to engage in the licentious worship of Baal and Ashtaroth, their omnipotent Protector would become their enemy, and they would soon fall a prey to the fierce, warlike nations around them. This plan was readily accepted by the king, and Balaam remained to assist in carrying it into effect."*[1] It is during this period of church history represented by Pergamus that the truths of Christianity were compromised for the purpose of bring hoards of unconverted pagans into the church. Compromise is a potent weapon in Satan's arsenal and he uses it with great skill in the ideological war against God's people.

In the experience of the church at Thyatira (Rev. 2:18-29), another ideological victory for Satan can be seen. *"You allow that woman Jezebel, who calls herself a prophetess, to teach and seduce My servants"* (Rev. 2:20). This experience in church history reflects the influence that Queen Jezebel had over ancient Israel. Not only did she lead

Israel into deeper apostasy, but she used the finances of the state to support her brand of religion. When Elijah challenged Ahab, Israel's apostate king, he said, *"'Now therefore, send and gather all Israel to me on Mount Carmel, the four hundred and fifty prophets of Baal, and the four hundred prophets of Asherah, who eat at Jezebel's table'"* (1 Kings 18:19). The teaching of Jezebel that entered the church promoted a church-state relationship. During the period of church history represented by Thyatira, the Roman Church became the dominating power over the political states in Europe.

When we reach the church of Laodicea (Rev. 3:14-22), seventh and last church in this prophecy, the condition of the Christian church is so tepid that Jesus threatens to vomit the church out of His mouth (Rev. 3:16).

In the struggle of the great controversy between John's day and the end of time, the seven churches present the major issues in the ideological war. Because the ideological war is terminated when Jesus returns, the prophecy of the seven churches goes no further while the prophecies of the seals and trumpets, which deal with the firefights, extend to the close of the millennium. But there is more to come, *i.e.*, the firefights.

Seven Seals

The prophecy of the seven seals has the longest introduction of any prophecy in Revelation. The location of this introductory scene is heaven. The Father is presented as sitting upon His throne holding a scroll sealed with seven seals (Rev. 4). The Lion of the tribe of Judah, a Lamb appearing as though it had been slain, takes the scroll from the hand of the Father and prepares to open it while the four living creatures, twenty-four elders, the angels, and the universe rendered praise to Him (Rev. 5). With the opening of the seals (Rev. 6-8:1), we are introduced to persecution and martyrdom—the firefights of the great controversy. The firefights pictured in the seals are all in-house. Inspired by the anger and rage of Satan, Christian persecuted and martyred Christian.

It is here that we find the four horsemen of the apocalypse. When the first seal is opened a rider on a white horse appears, the rider is given a bow and a στεφανος (crown of victory), and he rides forth to conquer (Rev. 6:1, 2). The white horse and its rider represents the early victories of the church within the pagan Roman Empire. These victories were gained by the preaching of the gospel and not by the sword. However, things change quickly. The first seal, so to speak, pictures the transition from the ideological phase of the controversy to the firefights. As Christianity was developing into the dominant religion in the empire, sinking deeper into apostasy and repeatedly compromising truth, it turned upon those Christians that rejected and reproved the error of its ways. Those who remained loyal to Jesus were persecuted and martyred. And as the next three horses appear—red, black, and pale—things within the church go from bad to worse (Rev. 6:3-8). Finally, when the fifth seal is opened, those who had been martyred in the firefights for their loyalty to truth cry out to God for revenge (Rev. 6:9-11).

With the opening of the sixth seal the scene changes again (Rev. 6:12-17). Responding to the cries for vengeance by the martyrs, God acts. The sixth seal is opened with the events in the natural world that Jesus said would be signs of His return (Mt. 24:29)—earthquake (sixth seal only), sun darkened, moon appears as blood, and the stars fall from heaven. Jesus said these events in nature would signal the close of the dark age tribulation . John sees these same events opening the sixth seal (Rev. 6:12, 13). Today we are living between the events reported in v. 13 and v. 14—the stars fall and the sky parts as a scroll when Jesus returns.

In the sixth seal, God gets involved in the firefights on behalf of His people. The sky parts as a scroll being rolled up as He approaches earth, there is a worldwide earthquake, the lost cry for the falling mountains to cover them and hide them so they will not have to look upon the face of God.

As the sixth seal pictures the devastation of Planet Earth by the massive earthquake, the Father is presented as accompanying Jesus to take vengeance upon those who persecute His people. Those who are lost cry to the rocks and mountains, *"Fall on us and hide us from the face of Him who sits on the throne and from the wrath of the Lamb!"* (Rev. 6:16). In the introduction to the seven seals, the One who sits upon the throne is the Father (Chapter 4), and the Lamb, of course, is Jesus (Chapter 5). This is why the oldest New Testament manuscripts read, *"For the great day of Their wrath has come"* in v 17 instead of *"His wrath"* which refers to the Lamb only.

Chapter 7 has been seen as an interlude or parenthesis between the sixth and seven seals. The silence in heaven for about half an hour mentioned in the seventh seal (Rev. 8:1) has been thought to picture one of two things. First, the vacancy within the heavenly courts as the Father, Son, and angels descend to earth to gather together the saints. But what does silence in vacant courts have to do with the great controversy? Or, second, others think this period of silence takes place as Jesus approaches the earth, and is what Ellen White describes in *The Great Controversy, "With anthems of celestial melody the holy angels, a vast, unnumbered throng attend Him on His way....The angels' song is hushed, and there is a period of awful silence. Then the voice of Jesus is heard, saying, 'My grace is sufficient for you.' The faces of the righteous are lighted up, and joy fills every heart."*[2]

Because Revelation is a book of apocalyptic prophecies, the half hour period must be seen as apocalyptic time, which is seven-and-a-half days. It is doubtful that during Jesus' return He and the angels will hover in the sky over the earth for over a week in "awful silence." It is also doubtful that the period of silence in the seventh seal is the result of the heavenly courts being vacated. Remember, each seal depicts separate and distinct action that is connected to the controversy. Seal six pictures action—the earth devastated by an earthquake, the lost running from the faces of the Father and the Son, mountains and rocks burying the lost. Why would seal seven picture silence in heavenly courts or the angels hovering over the earth in "awful silence" because of the action taking place in seal six? To be consistent, seal seven must depict some kind of action that is not connected to any previous seal.

Would it be helpful if we did not think of Rev. 7 as an interlude, but, rather, as the closing scene of the sixth seal? As the mountains bury the lost, they cry out, *"The great day of [Their] wrath has come, and who is able to stand?"* (Rev. 6:17). The answer to the question posed by the lost is found in Chapter 7. Those who will live through this traumatic experience are sealed by God—the 144,000 (Rev. 7:1-8). They will be able to stand. The scene in Chapter 7 is then expanded to include a great multitude from all the nations of the earth who are clothed with white robes, holding palm branches, and giving praise to *"God who sits on the throne, and to the Lamb"* (Rev. 7:10). Here are the 144,000 and the redeemed of all ages before the throne, those who will be led by the Lamb to the living fountains of water (Rev. 7:17).

This heavenly scene in Chapter 7 follows the thematic flow of events and is a glimpse of the experience of the redeemed following the return of Jesus. It is a snapshot of their experience during the millennium. When the 1,000 years are finished, the seventh seal is opened and it is filled with action. The seventh seal presents the final event in the great controversy, *"When He opened the seventh seal, there was silence in heaven for about half an hour."* The seventh seal includes the final firefight in the great controversy which is detailed in Rev. 20. When the lost are raised to stand in the White-Throne Judgment, Satan marshals his demons and the lost for the final engagement with Christ and His followers in battle four. They surround the Holy City and fire comes down from heaven and destroys them all. As the universe witnesses the close of the controversy, all singing and praises being given to God cease. The universe watches in hushed awe as God performs a strange work, a strange act (Isa. 28:21). The One who is the source of life destroys life and what He has created, a destruction that involves the whole earth (Isa. 28:22). So there will be silence in heaven for about half an hour (a little over a week) as the purifying flames do their work.

There was a previous time in the great controversy when silence was experienced in heaven. It was when Jesus made the ultimate sacrifice for sinful man. Ellen White descries it this way, *"And there was silence in heaven; no harp was touched. Could mortals have viewed the amazement of the angelic host as they watched in silent grief the Father separating His beams of light, love, and glory, from the beloved Son, they would better understand how offensive sin is in His sight."*[3] Silence in heaven twice—1) the death of God's Son, and 2) the destruction of all sinners, including Lucifer and his demons. On both of these occasions, the silence does not result from heaven being empty, but because the universe watches God carry out a strange act that will never be repeated.

Seven Trumpets

While the seven churches prophesy the progressive stages of apostasy within the Christian Church, or the ideological war, and the seven seals prophesy the in-house firefights, the seven trumpets prophesy God's attempt to bring an apostate church back to Himself by allowing firefights to be inflicted upon the Christian world from sources outside the church.

The reader is taken back to the heavenly sanctuary for the introduction to this prophecy (Rev. 8:2-6). Seven angels are given seven trumpets. An eighth angel puts fire from the altar of incense into his censer and when he has added much incense he throws the censer into the earth and the angels sound their trumpets.

As the Roman Empire began to crack and collapse under the weight of its own moral decay and the church adopted pagan beliefs as a compromise to gain converts and earthly power, God tried to bring the church back to biblical truth. By using marauding pagan armies, an apostate church was exposed to the judgments of God. Blowing of trumpets in the Bible represent the approach of judgment and/or war. As Jesus said concerning the church at Thyatira, *"I gave her time to repent..., and she did not repent"* (Rev. 2:21).

Some see a parallel between the seven trumpets and the seven last plagues and conclude that the plagues are a restatement of the trumpets. Although there may be parallels in the prophetic imagery, they are not one and the same. The first six trumpets are a part of the events of the great controversy that take place during the third battle presented in Revelation 12. Only the seventh trumpet is a part of battle four. By contrast, all of the seven last plagues are a part of the firefights in battle four. Trumpet five that prophesies the first onslaught of Islam upon Christianity in Palestine, North Africa, and Spain has a time prophecy connected to it. Trumpet six that prophesies the fall of the Byzantine Empire before the attack of the Muslim Turks also has a time prophecy. The time in trumpet five is five months (Rev. 9:5) or 150 years. The time in trumpet six is a day, a month, and a year (Rev. 9:15) or 391 years thus giving a total of 541 years between the two trumpets. On the basis of these time prophecies, it is clear that the seven trumpets and the seven plagues are not one and the same. While the fifth and sixth trumpets have a total time of 541 years connected to them, the plagues that fall upon spiritual Babylon will come in one prophetic day, or approximately one year (Rev. 18:8).

Chapters 10 and 11 are true interludes between the sixth and seventh trumpets. In these two chapters two significant events in the great controversy are prophesied. Chapter 10 pictures John eating the open book which he received from the angel's hand. As he eats, the book is sweet in his mouth but bitter in his stomach. With this prophetic imagery, God prophesies the rise of His remnant church and their mission, *"You must prophesy again to many peoples, nations, tongues, and kings"* (Rev. 10:11). Chapter 11 pictures Satan's attempt to take the Bible out of the hands of the people, but this attempt gives rise to modern Bible societies which have multiplied copies of God's word by the millions and have made the Bible available to people around the world.

At the blowing of the seventh trumpet, the kingdoms of this world become the kingdoms of Christ. The nations are angry, the time of God's wrath has come, the dead are judged, the saints receive their reward, and Christ will destroy those who destroy the earth (Rev. 11:18).

With these three prophecies extending from Chapter 1 to the end of Chapter 11, the experience of the church and the unfolding of the great controversy between Christ and Satan from John's day to the end are presented. By recapitulation, detail is added to detail in this broad sweep of battles three and four in the history of the church.

Now the thematic structure of Revelation changes. As we have seen, Chapter 12 introduces the great controversy with four battles. Battle four is presented in one verse, *"The dragon was enraged with the woman and went to make war with the rest [remnant] of her off-spring"* (Rev. 12:17). The rest of Revelation, except for the two concluding chapters, expands and explains this one verse—how the war against God's end-time people will be fought.

Reference

1. White, Ellen G. *Patriarchs and Prophets*, Mountain View, CA, Pacific Press Publishing Association, (1913), p. 451.

2. _____, *The Great Controversy*, p. 641.

3. _____, *Signs of the Times*, December 8, 1897.

Chapter Four

It's War!

I will never forget one of the first Bible studies that I gave as a ministerial intern. The senior pastor had given me several cards with names and addresses of people who might prove to be possible interests. As I made the visits, I found an elderly couple who had recently moved from Poland to the United States. The gentleman was interested in personal Bible studies and I was ecstatic. We moved from topic to topic with little difficulty until we came to Rev. 13. He had no problem with the sea beast representing the papacy. I remember thinking to myself, if he, being from Poland, has no problem with the sea beast representing the papacy, we have got it made. However, when we came to the land beast in Rev. 13, my ecstasy was dashed to pieces. When he discovered that the United States was presented as a political power that would become intolerant, take away religious freedom, and force its will upon the people, he threw up his hands in horror. He had lived through the Nazi and Russian occupations of Poland, and he was convinced that the United States would never put its citizens through what he had experienced in the land of his birth. Our Bible studies ended abruptly, and I was left in a daze not knowing what to do or say. My problem was that I had not laid a firm enough foundation by studying Rev. 12 first. Once you understand Chapter 12, especially

12:17, what is presented in Rev. 13 becomes feasible.

If you were to open up the Book of Revelation for the first time and at random turn to any chapter between 13 and 20, your head would probably begin to swim and you would lay the Bible down and say, "Revelation is not a book for me!" But really, the last half of Revelation is not that difficult. Having read the two previous chapters in *Revelation and the Great Controversy*, the last half of Revelation will make sense. Let's review for a minute what you have already read.

Chapter 12 is the center around which Revelation's prophecies revolve. This chapter presents the great controversy between Christ and Satan in the form of four battles. Two were complete when John began to write, the third battle occupies the major portion of the content in Rev. 1 to 11 (seven churches, seven seals, and seven trumpets) and deals with the ideological war between truth and error as well as the bloodshed resulting from persecution during the history of the Christian church.

The fourth and final battle is contained in the last verse of Rev. 12, *"And the dragon was enraged with the woman, and he went to make war with the rest [remnant] of her offspring, who keep the commandments of God and have the testimony of Jesus Christ"* (v. 17). The remainder of Revelation, except for the last two chapters, is an expansion and explanation of this one verse, i.e., how battle four will be fought.

The reason Satan is enraged with the remnant people of God is because they are obedient to God and keep His commandments. Satan is also enraged with them because they have the prophetic gift that unmasks his military strategy and gives a deeper insight as to how this final battle will be fought as well as the issues that will be involved in the battle. With this information and the guidance of the Holy Spirit, the remnant are equipped to resist his deceptions.

When the Holy Spirit inspired John to write that Satan was enraged with God's remnant people and was determined to make war on them, He was not overstating the case. Satan hates the remnant who keep God's commandments. As Roger Morneau shares his experience of finding biblical truth, he relates a portion of a telephone conversation he had with his friend Roland. Roger and Roland had been preparing for indoctrination into a satanic cult when God intervened and rescued Roger. Having taken 28 Bible studies in one week, having missed the indoctrination ceremony, and having gone to church on the Sabbath for the first time, Satan was angry.

As Roger and Roland talked on the phone after Roger's first day in church, Roland communicated the anger of Satan, *"On Tuesday night, during the sacred hour of midnight, a spirit counselor appeared to him [the satanic priest] and told him that you were studying the Bible with Sabbath keepers, the very people the master hates most on the face of the earth."*[1]

As the conversation continued, Roland said, *"At 6:30 this evening the high priest called to inform me that according to the spirits you have been in church today with those Sabbath people, and that has infuriated the master."*[2]

Finishing his phone conversation with Roland, Roger entered his apartment where a spirit counselor was waiting for him, *"'Listen to me carefully,' the spirit said. 'I am telling you the truth. The master has great wealth prepared for you if only you give up associating with the people he hates, and stop observing that Seventh-day Sabbath he despises.'"*[3]

In battle four, we are shown how Satan plots with his supporters to rid the earth of all who follow Christ and keep His commandments. The very people Satan hates the most. It's war!

Satan's military strategy

Rev. 13 exposes Satan's military strategy for battle four. In this chapter we find the following: 1) a coalition will be formed between two world powers, the sea beast and the land beast; 2) the land beast will force those who live on the earth to give worship and homage to the sea beast (v. 12); it will also 3) cause an image to the sea beast to be formed (v. 14); and 4) cause the mark of the sea beast's authority to be placed upon peoples' foreheads or right hands (v. 16); 5) those who will not render obedience to the image of the beast will be placed under a death decree (v. 15); and 6) those who refuse the mark of the beast will be placed under an economic ban (v. 17).

Rev. 14 to 20 reveals God's battle plan. God meets Satan's military strategy ideological point by ideological point, blow by blow, firefight by firefight and gains the victory for His people.

The sea beast

According to Rev. 12:17, the fourth and final battle will be a war waged against God's remnant people. A battle that is to be fought at the climax of earth's history. The introduction of the sea beast in Rev. 13:1-10 is a historical review for the reader's benefit and lays the foundation for the coalition between the two world powers. The sea beast has been around for centuries, and is represented in Daniel 7 and 8 by horns. Through the power that is represented by the sea beast, Satan waged war against the followers of Jesus in battle three. This power represented by the prophetic symbols of horns in Daniel 7 and 8 and a beast coming up out of the sea in Rev. 13 is the papacy.

Notice the similarities between the horns in Daniel and the sea beast in Revelation.

Dan. 7	Dan. 8	Rev. 13
Speaks pompous words (vv. 8, 11, 20, 25)	Exalts self to the Prince of the Host (v. 11)	Speaks great things and blasphemes (vv. 5, 6)
	Casts God's sanctuary down (v. 12)	Blasphemes God's tabernacle (v. 6)
Saints given into his hands (v. 25)		Makes war with saints and overcomes them (v. 6)
Persecutes saints for a time, times, and half a time (v. 25)		Continues 42 months (v. 5)

The prophetic time of 1,260 years during which this blasphemous power makes war on God's people is the connecting link that places this power squarely within battle three. In Dan. 7, the saints were given into the hands of the horn power for a time, times, and half a time (v. 25). In Rev. 13, the sea beast makes war with the saints and was given authority to continue for 42 months (v. 7, 5). In Rev. 12, during battle three, God's people flee into the wilderness where they are nourished for 1,260 years (v. 6) and for a time, times, and a half of time (v. 14). The two appearances of this time prophecy within the description of battle three does two things. First, it establishes without a doubt where this prophetic period belongs in the chronology of the great controversy, and, second, ties the horn of Dan. 7 and the sea beast of Rev. 13 to the time and events described in battle three.

The appearance of the sea beast at the beginning of battle four is not an introduction of a new power into world history. Rather its presence helps the reader to see the makeup of the coalition that will be fighting against God's remnant.

It might be helpful to pause for a moment to help those who are not familiar with prophetic time periods. In apocalyptic prophecy, a day is equal to one year (Num. 14:34, Ezek. 4:6). Therefore 1,260

41

days is 1,260 years. Forty-two months is 42 x30 (30 days in a month according to the ancient Jewish lunar calendar) or 1,260 days or years. A time equals one year, times is two years, and a half of time is half a year thus giving three and one-half times or years. Because apocalyptic prophecy always goes from days to years, the three and one-half years must be reduced to days. One year (a time) has 360 days (Jewish lunar calendar), two years (times) has 720 days, and a half a year (one-half a time) has 180 days which equals 1,260 days or years. Which is the time period during which the horn/sea beast wars against God's people in battle three.

Now, back to the sea beast of Rev. 13. This power, as noted above, has been around for centuries and has been used as an instrument by Satan in his war against God's people. Now in Rev. 13, the papacy assumes a new role in the great controversy as it teams up with the land beast to fight battle four. In other words, to fully understand what Satan's strategy will be in battle four, it is necessary at the beginning of Chapter 13 for a quick historical review so we can get a better picture of what he is planning in his war against the remnant, *i.e.*, the sea beast, an old, established power, will enter into league with a new, energetic power, the land beast, in order to carry out Satan's military strategy.

The land beast

The beast with the two lamb-like horns that rises up out of the land (Rev. 13:11-18) represents the United States. John probably saw an American bison, an animal that he was not acquainted with, therefore he could not identify it. He was able to identify the body parts of the sea beast because he was familiar with the animals, a body like a leopard, feet like a bear, and a mouth like a lion (Rev. 13:2). When the land beast uses its vocal cords it roars like a dragon.

The identity of the land beast and its role in Satan's military plans for the final conflict is clearly stated by Ellen White, *"It has been shown that the United States is the power represented by the beast with lamb-like horns, and that this prophecy will be fulfilled when the United States shall enforce Sunday observance, which Rome claims as the special acknowledgment of her supremacy."*[4] This understanding of the land beast was more than what our friend from Poland could tolerate.

The formation of the image to the sea beast and the enforcement of its mark of authority by the land beast fulfills Satan's great ambition. Satan is the original antichrist, as we have seen. The papacy is his representative in the Christian world, thus the Christian antichrist. Remember that the meaning of the word antichrist is to take the place of Christ. As homage, worship, and obedience are given to papal authority, the homage, worship, and obedience that should go to Christ are diverted through the papacy to Satan who stands behind his earthly representative. This is explained by John, *"So they worshiped the dragon who gave authority to the beast; and they worshiped the beast"* (Rev. 13:4). The older Greek manuscripts have an interesting variant reading, *"So they worshiped the dragon because he gave authority to the beast; and they worshiped the beast"* (emphasis added).

Ellen White says further, *"The worship of images and relics, the invocation of saints, and the exaltation of the pope, are devices of Satan to attract the minds of the people from God and from His Son."*[5]

Unfortunately the United States by forming the image to the beast and enforcing Sunday will be foremost in leading the world in worshiping or giving obedience to the sea beast. John says of the land beast, *"And he exercises all the authority of the first beast in his presence, and causes the earth and those who dwell in it to worship the first beast, whose deadly wound was healed"* (Rev. 13:12).

Now for a closer look at Satan's military strategy. It is divided into the two phases of warfare that we have become acquainted with. First the ideological phase: Protestant churches by pressuring political leaders to enact laws that will further their agenda will establish a church-state working relationship. This church-state relationship will reflect the characteristics of the sea beast, thus we have the image to the beast. The lobbying and pressure on law makers will spark an intense debate. This debate will be open for all to follow and will involve the opinions of the people on the streets. The evening news, the talk shows, the press, and the internet will be the places where the ideological war will be fought. Those pressuring congress for the active role of religion in government will finally win the day.

The ideological war will also include public pressure for a national Sunday law, the mark of the sea beast. This issue will also be debated in congress and by the public. It is at this time, when Sunday becomes a national issue, that the third angel's message of Rev. 14:9-11 will produce results in the United States and around the world that God's remnant people have not witnessed before.

"Heretofore those who presented the truths of the third angel's message have often been regarded as mere alarmists. Their predictions that religious intolerance would gain control in the United States, that church and state would unite to persecute those who keep the commandments of God, have been pronounced groundless and absurd. It has been confidently declared that this land could never become other than what it has been,—the defender of religious freedom. But as the question of enforcing Sunday observance is widely agitated, the event so long doubted and disbelieved is seen to be approaching and the third message will produce an effect which it could not have had before."[6]

At the time of this writing, articles have already appeared in the press such as *Time*, *WORLD*, *Christianity Today*, and *Guideposts* supporting the sacredness of Sunday and lamenting the violation of the sacredness of Sunday by businesses who open on the "Christian sabbath." The ideological war leading up to the formation of the image to the beast and the Sunday law will not be fought in secret. Arguments from both sides will be open for all to hear and consider.

Now the firefights. Those who refuse to worship or obey the image of the beast will be placed under a death decree (Rev. 13:15). Those who refuse to receive the mark of the sea beast will be placed under an economic ban (Rev. 13:17). It's war!

People have wondered for many years how an economic ban will be placed on those who refuse to receive the mark of the beast. Now at least three possibilities present themselves. 1) The issuing of national identity cards, 2) bioimplants which have now been approved by the FDA, and 3) a new development by the Japanese, identification by the iris of the eye. Since 9/11 pressure has been mounting for some means of securing our country from infiltrators who wish to do Americans harm. Bioimplants, a computer chip with all of a person's vital information and identity placed under the skin, can accomplish this plus making possible a goal that some have advocated for years, a cashless society. It is believed that a cashless society will stop drug sales, bank robberies, fraud, etc. With a computer chip implant all financial transactions can be done electronically. Electronic transactions can be monitored and manipulated by the government and people can be put in a position where they will not be able to buy or sell. Scanning the iris of the eye can work in a similar way to produce a cashless society.

Ellen White gives a summary of the ideological and firefight phases in battle four with the following words, *"Through the two great errors, the immortality of the soul and Sunday sacredness, Satan will bring the people under his deceptions. While the former lays the foundation of Spiritualism, the latter creates a bond of sympathy with Rome. The Protestants of the United States will be foremost in stretching their hands across the gulf to grasp the hand of Spiritualism; they will reach over the abyss to clasp hands with the Roman power, and under the influence of this threefold union, this country will follow in the steps of Rome in trampling on the rights of conscience."*[7] Our Polish friend threw up his hands when presented with this fact.

Sunday law

There are four basic issues that will lead congress to enact a Sunday law.

1. The moral decay of this nation will be seen as a threat to its welfare. We have already seen a growing reaction among evangelicals to this nation's moral slide in the formation of the Ten Commandment Commission and the designation of the first Sunday in May as Ten Commandment Sunday. There is a call going out to bring this nation back to a recognition that the keeping of God's law is the foundation of its strength and prosperity. We are told that eventually this moral decay will be seen as a result of the desecration of the sacredness of Sunday. Religious leaders *"will put forth the claim that the fast-spreading corruption is largely attributable to the desecration of the so-called 'Christian sabbath,' and that the enforcement of Sunday observance would greatly improve the morals of society."*[8]

2. National disasters, man-made, natural, and financial upheaval will be on the increase. These disasters will be viewed as a sign of God's displeasure because of the moral decay in society and the desecration of Sunday. Respecting the sacredness of Sunday will be seen as a way of appeasing God's anger. *"It*

will be declared that men are offending God by the violation of the Sunday-sabbath; that this sin has brought calamities which will not cease until Sunday observance shall be strictly enforced; and that those who present the claims of the fourth commandment, thus destroying reverence for Sunday, are troublers of the people, preventing their restoration to divine favor and temporal prosperity."[9]

3. Commandment keepers will be seen as enemies of the nation because they resist the idea of the civil enforcement of Sunday. Obedience to civil law is seen as being ordained by God. *"Those who honor the Bible Sabbath will be denounced as enemies of law and order, as breaking down the moral restraints of society, causing anarchy and corruption, and calling down the judgments of God upon the earth....Ministers who deny the obligation of the divine law will present from the pulpit the duty of yielding obedience to the civil authorities as ordained by God."*

"Political corruption is destroying love of justice and regard for truth; and even in free America, rulers and legislators, in order to secure public favor, will yield to the popular demand for a law enforcing Sunday observance."[10]

4. As the proposed Sunday law is openly debated, the biblical evidence for God's Sabbath will be clearly stated and seen. Having never thought this evidence through before, honest seekers for truth will go to their ministers and ask them why the church keeps Sunday when Scripture clearly says Saturday is God's Sabbath. The clergy have no biblical evidence for Sunday. They are enraged at being challenged and this only motivates them further to silence the opposition by enacting a national law. *"But since many refuse to be satisfied with the*

*mere authority of men, and demand a plain 'Thus saith the
Lord,' the popular ministry, like the Pharisees of old, filled
with anger as their authority is questioned, will denounce the
[third angel's] message as of Satan, and stir up the sin-loving
multitudes to revile and persecute those who proclaim it.* "[11]

Within the context of this ideological war over a national Sunday
law, people take sides. John says that those who accept the mark of
the beast receive it either in their foreheads or their right hands (Rev.
13:16). This mark, of course, is not a visible mark or a brand. The
forehead represents an intellectual acceptance of the Sunday law. The
right hand indicates that a person may not agree with the law, but he
goes along with it to save his neck.

The United States has proven to be one of the greatest nations in
human history. It has developed into a world power that grants political and religious freedom to its people. It has been a haven of refuge
for the oppressed. It has come to the aide of other nations at a great
cost to itself. But when it uses its power to bring people into obedience
to the wishes and teaching of the sea beast, disaster lies at the door.
Here are two predictions of the fate of the United States when it will
form an image to the sea beast and enforces a national Sunday law.

*"When the Protestant churches shall unite with the secular power
to sustain a false religion, for opposing which their ancestors endured
the fiercest persecution; when the state shall use its power to enforce
the decrees and sustain the institutions of the church, then will Protestant America have formed an image to the papacy, and there will be a
national apostasy which will end only in national ruin."* [12]

A similar statement is made regarding the enactment and enforcement of a national Sunday law.

*"When our nation, in its legislative councils, shall enact laws to
bind the consciences of men in regard to their religious privileges,*

enforcing Sunday observance, and bringing oppressive power to bear against those who keep the seventh-day Sabbath, the law of God will, to all intents and purposes, be made void in our land , and national apostasy will be followed by national ruin. "[13]

National ruin! It's hard to visualize such a thing in the future of the United States. It's war! And the Holy Spirit unfolds before us Satan's military strategy for battle four in Rev. 13. God's strategy for fighting this battle is given to us in the remaining chapters of Revelation. Although the issues involved are spiritual, theological, and faith-based, the battle is real none-the-less.

References

1. Morneau, p. 12

2. Ibid., p. 13

3. Ibid., p. 14

4. White, *The Great Controversy, p. 579.*

5. Ibid., p. 568.

6. Ibid., pp. 605-06.

7. Ibid., p. 588.

8. Ibid., p. 587.

9. Ibid., p. 590.

10. Ibid., p. 592.

11. Ibid., p. 607.

12. White, *Seventh-day Adventist Commentary*, vol. 7, p. 976.

13. Ibid., p. 977.

Chapter Five

Jesus' Counter-Offensive: The Ideological War

Have you ever read about Martin Luther and the ink bottle? When the reformer stood before Emperor Charles V and the papal delegation at the Diet of Worms, he was asked if he would retract his writings against the papal system and the abuses that existed in the Roman Catholic Church. Even though he knew that they were thirsting for his blood, he refused to back down and spoke those famous words as he pointed to his books, "Here I stand. God help me! Amen." The emperor had given Luther a three week safe conduct to get back to his home at the University of Wittenberg where he taught theology. After the three weeks Luther was to be declared an outlaw and could be put to death by anyone who found him. The Elector Frederick, under whose jurisdiction Luther lived and at whose university he taught, feared that Luther's enemies would not wait out the three weeks. So he arranged for the secret kidnaping of Luther, and he was spirited away to the fortress called "The Wartburg." During the following months of isolation Luther translated the Greek New Testament into German. Tradition has it that while hard at work on his translation, the shadow of Satan appeared on the wall of his room in front of him. Luther, seeing the shadow, picked up the ink bottle at his side and threw it at Satan. The bottle shattered against the wall and splattered ink all over the shadow. How many times have you wished you could throw something at Satan?

In Rev. 14-20, God "throws the book" at Satan for us. If you are just beginning the study of the Book of Revelation, an understanding of Satan' military strategy as presented in Chapter 13 will help you get a handle on Chapter 14. Beginning with Rev. 14, Jesus shows John how He is going to win each of the two phases of battle four. We have seen that Rev. 13 maps out Satan's military strategy. In phase one the enemy fights an ideological war against the remnant through the formation of the image of the beast and the establishment of the mark of the beast. His strategy for phase two, physical engagement, is the death decree and an economic ban. Now Rev. 14 shows us how Jesus engages the enemy in the ideological war and wins the victory. Jesus' victory in the firefights will be dealt with in the following chapters. In both phases of engagement in the great controversy, God "throws the book at Satan."

144,000

Before giving the details as to how the ideological victory will be won, the 144,000 appear once again (Rev. 14:1-5). We first met them within the context of the Father's and Jesus' approach to Planet Earth as it is convulsed by a devastating earthquake (Rev. 6:15, 16). As the lost cry out for the rocks and mountains to fall on them, they say, *"For the great day of [Their] wrath has come, and who is able to stand?"* (Rev. 6:17). The answer to this question is given in the Chapter 7, the 144, 000.

With the appearance of the 144,000 at the beginning of Chapter 14, one wonders if the Holy Spirit is leading John to follow the sequence found in the sixth seal—a traumatic experience (earthquake and appearance of the Father and the Son) that leads to a question ("Who will be able to stand?") and then an answer (the 144,000). Although the reader will not find the question posed at the end of Chapter 13 as it appears at the end of Chapter 6, it is asked in connection with the description of the sea beast. As the whole earth is led to give worship and obedience to the sea beast through Satan's lies, the arrogant question is asked by those who sell themselves out to Satan's deceptions, *"Who is like the beast? Who is able to make war with him?"* (Rev. 13:4). The answer now becomes clear, Jesus in the person of the 144,000 (Rev. 14:1-5). By His strength and grace, they are the victors in the ideological war.

They have made a clear, deliberate, and intellectual decision to stand with Jesus in battle four. Those who receive the mark of the beast have this mark in their foreheads or on their right hands. The 144,000, by contrast, have the Father's name written in their foreheads only (Rev. 14:1). Whereas those who receive the mark of the beast may agree intellectually to render obedience to the sea beast or may not intellectually agree with the mark but render obedience to save their necks, this approach cannot be taken with God. The name of the Father is written in the forehead only. God does not accept any right-hand worship.

Jesus' Counter-Offensive in the Ideological War

Jesus counters Satan's lies and deception in the ideological war with the three angels' messages of Rev. 14:6-11. This counter-offensive against error is pictured as three angels flying in the midst of heaven proclaiming the final warning to a doomed world. These messages go *"to those who dwell on the earth—to every nation, tribe, tongue, and people"* (Rev. 14:6), to the very ones whom the land beast tries to lead to give worship and obedience to the sea beast (Rev. 13:12).

First Angels' Message. The first angel's message is the first part of Jesus' ideological counter-offensive. This message is divided into two parts. The first is a warning that a preadvent, investigative judgment has already begun in heaven. The 2,300 year prophecy of Dan. 8:14 and its interpretation found in Dan. 9:24-27 lie at the foundation of this warning. To understand how these two passages are connected is crucial because Dan. 9:24-27 has been separated from 8:14 and has been used to defend the teaching of seven years of tribulation after the secret rapture during which the antichrist is supposed to arise.

But this teaching cannot be defended, therefore it is important that a few minutes be spent looking at Daniel's prophecy so we will not be taken in by the error of the secret rapture. Dan. 8:14 speaks of 2,300 evenings and mornings or days. In apocalyptic prophecy this is 2,300 years. Gabriel told Daniel in 8:26 that the vision (*mareh*, one of two Hebrew words for vision) of the evenings and mornings (referring back to 8:14) is true. When Gabriel gave to Daniel the interpretation of the 2,300 years in the next chapter, he told Daniel, *"therefore consider the matter, and understand the vision"* (Dan. 9:23). The word for vision in this verse is *mareh* and thus 8:14, 8:26, and 9:23 are linked together. Gabriel directed Daniel's mind back to the 2,300 years of 8:14 and was now ready to give him its meaning in 9:24-27.

In Gabriel's explanation, a period of 70 weeks (or 490 prophetic years) is cut off from the first part of the 2,300 years in order to accomplish the numerous things listed in Dan. 9:24. This 70 weeks or 490 years is then subdivided into a 69 week period (or 483 prophetic years, Dan. 9:25), thus leaving one week (or 7 prophetic years) between the end of the 69 weeks and the end of the 70 weeks. The 69 weeks and the 70 weeks have the same starting point in history. At the end of the 69 weeks *"Messiah the Prince"* would appear (Dan. 9:25). This leaves one week or 7 years for the completion of the 70 weeks. In the middle of this prophetic week the Messiah would be cut off and the sacrifices and offerings would be brought to an end (Jesus' crucifixion, Dan. 9:26, 27).

The 2,300 years began with the command of the Persian king Artaxerxes in 457 B.C. to rebuild Jerusalem (Dan. 9:25) and ended in 1844

A.D. The 70 weeks and the 69 weeks are the first part of the 2,300 years and cannot be separated from them. Following the 70 weeks or 490 years, there remains 1,810 years to complete the 2,300 years. Which brings us to 1844 A.D. At this time the preadvent, investigative judgment began being represented by "the cleansing of the sanctuary" in Dan. 8:14. As we know from the services in the Old Testament earthly sanctuary, this cleansing process took place on the Day of Atonement and was known as a day of judgment (Lev. 16). The judgment in heaven is shown to us in Dan 7:9, 10 where thrones are put in place, the Ancient of Days takes His seat, the court is assembled, and the books are opened.

Based on the use of the Hebrew word *mareh*, a connection is formed between Dan 8:14, 8:26, and 9:23. It is impossible to say that the one prophetic week between the end of the 69 weeks and the end of the 70 weeks comes at the conclusion of earth's history, is the period of seven years of tribulation, and is the time during which the antichrist arises because following the 70 weeks or 490 years there remains 1,810 years to complete the time period in Dan. 8:14—the 2,300 years.

Based on this prophecy in Dan. 8:14, the first angel gives the warning to the world that the judgment which will decide the destiny of men has already begun. It is with this message that Jesus begins "throwing the book" at Satan and opens His counter-offensive in the ideological phase of battle four.

The second part of the first angel's message is a call to worship the Creator (Rev. 14:7) instead of the sea beast and the satanic power behind it. Inseparably tied to worshiping the Creator is the day set aside as a memorial of Jesus' great creative act—the seventh-day Sabbath.

In order for the call to return to the worship of the Creator and to keep His Sabbath to catch the attention of people, the theory of evolution will have to be openly challenged. People must have enough information to make an intelligent choice between the biblical account of the origin of life and Satan's lie about the origin of life. Once the debate between creation and evolution is easily accessible to the public, the seventh-day Sabbath will make sense to those who are willing to accept it.

There are at least five reasons why Saturday, the seventh-day Sabbath, is to be kept not only by Christians but all mankind. Each of them are grounded in Scripture and Jesus Himself is their foundation.

1. *Creation*: The first reason is tied directly to the creation of Planet Earth and the origin of life on this planet. After six 24 hour days of creation, the Creator rested from His work on the seventh day. As a memorial of His work, He blessed the seventh day and sanctified it (Gen. 2:1-3). Jesus is identified as the Creator (John 1:1-3, 10: Col. 1:15-17; Heb. 1:1-3). Saturday, the seventh day, was Jesus' personal choice as a memorial in time of His creative power and as a sacred day of rest for humans.

2. *Recreation*: When Jesus died on the cross, He made possible the restoration or recreation of sinful man. This work of grace is based on two great recreative acts, 1) His crucifixion on Friday, and 2) His resurrection on Sunday. Jesus rested in the tomb on the Sabbath between these two acts of recreation (Luke 23:53-24:3) just as He rested from His original work of creation on Saturday, the seventh day. Paul recognizes Jesus' work of recreation when he told the Corinthian Christians, *"Therefore, if anyone is in Christ, he is a new creation"* (2 Cor. 5:17).

3. *Sabbath kept in heaven.* The Old Testament prophet Isaiah tells us that after sin is destroyed and earth is made new again, the redeemed of all ages will observe the seventh-day Sabbath (Isa. 66:22, 23). There is no time in the history of mankind when Jesus set aside or abolished the memorial of His creative and recreative work—not in Old Testament times, not in New

Testament times, not today, nor will He set it aside through endless ages of eternity. The endless continuation of the seventh-day Sabbath illustrates the truth found in Heb. 13:8, *"Jesus Christ is the same yesterday, today, and forever."*

4. *Ten commandments*: The fourth commandment of God's holy law clearly states that the seventh day has been set aside since creation as a day of rest, a day that has been blessed and hallowed (Ex. 20:8-11). Paul tells us that it was Jesus who spoke this law at Sinai and gave it to Israel. First he says that the law was given through the hand of a Mediator (Gal. 3:19), and then says that there is only one Mediator between God and man, *"the Man Christ Jesus"* (1 Tim. 2:15).

Further evidence that Jesus is the law Giver is embedded within the Ten Commandments themselves. As Jesus concluded the debate with the religious leaders that is recorded in John 8, He said. *"'Most assuredly, I say to you, before Abraham was, I AM'"* (v. 58). I AM is the personal name of the Old Testament covenant God. Jesus identified Himself as that God. From the burning bush Moses heard the words, *"'Thus you shall say to the children of Israel, "I AM has sent me to you"'"* (Ex. 3:14). The I AM in Scripture is Jesus and His name in Hebrew is YHWH (from the Hebrew verb "to be").

This following bit of information found in the introduction to my NKJV (1992, Thomas Nelson Publishers) is interesting, *"The covenant name of God in the Old Testament, represented by the Hebrew consonants YHWH, is translated 'Lord' or 'God' (using capital letters as shown), as it has been throughout the history of the King James Bible."* Have you ever noticed that the Ten Commandments were introduced to Moses with the following words, *"I am the Lord your God, who brought you out of the land of Egypt?"* (Ex. 20:2) It was YHWH (Jehovah) or Jesus, the I AM, who brought the children of Israel to the promised land,

and it was Jesus who gave them the ten commandment law on the way. Reading through the Ten Commandments, "LORD" appears five times. Within the fourth commandment the following statement is found, *"but the seventh day is the Sabbath of the LORD your God"* (Ex. 20:10). The seventh-day is Jesus' Sabbath, not the Jewish Sabbath.

The seventh-day Sabbath is a memorial of Jesus' creative act and remains as evidence that Jesus owns this world and all living forms in it, it is a sign that He alone purges us from sin and prepares us for heaven, and it is part of His eternal law. This is why Satan hates the Sabbath. It contradicts all of his lies and deceptions in the ideological war that he is fighting against truth. This is why, also, he hates those who accept the seventh-day Sabbath.

5. *Sanctification*: Since Jesus is the God of the Old Testament as well as the New, throughout the history of sin salvation and purification have come only through Him. The following verse from Exodus is an illustration of this fact, *"'Surely My Sabbaths you shall keep, for it is a sign between Me and you throughout your generations, that you may know that I am the LORD who sanctifies you"* (Ex. 31:13; cf, Ezk. 20: 12). The seventh-day Sabbath is not only a memorial of Jesus' creative work, it is also a sign of sanctification or purification from sin by YHWH, the I AM, even in the Old Testament. This is the offer of grace. Paul points out that there is only one way sanctification can be achieved, *"Therefore Jesus also, that He might sanctify the people with His own blood, suffered outside the gate"* (Heb. 13:12). Therefore the observance of the seventh-day Sabbath is a testimony that we have accepted the blood of Jesus for the forgiveness of our sins.

These five reasons for keeping the biblical Sabbath are grounded in Jesus. You cannot separate the seventh-day Sabbath from Him. If you do away with one, you do away with the other. The truth of Jesus' creative acts and the seventh-day Sabbath as a memorial of His creative power is the second part of the first angel's message which, in turn, is the opening of Jesus' counter-offensive in the ideological war.

Second angel's message. The second part of Jesus' ideological counter-offensive is the warning that spiritual Babylon is in a fallen condition (Rev. 14:8). The word "Babylon" comes from the Old Testament account of "Babel," the tower that was to reach to heaven and was to become a refuge for sinful man if there was another flood, and from the confusion of languages when God stepped in and stopped its construction. In Revelation, Babylon represents the various forms of false or apostate religions, mainly the various Christian churches that have given up biblical truth and have accepted the errors of Satan. Babylon is represented as a harlot that is drunken on the blood of the saints in Rev. 17:1-6 and as a city in Rev. 18. When we will look at Jesus' counter-offensive to Satan's firefights, we will see that the city of Babylon is made up of three entities—the dragon, the beast, and the false prophet (Rev. 16:13), and when Jesus gains the victory, Babylon falls into three parts (Rev. 16:19).

The messages of the three angels are sequential. Connected to the first angel's message is the rise of the advent movement under the preaching of William Miller and the message of preadvent judgment. This, historically, was followed by the discovery of the biblical evidence supporting the seventh-day Sabbath. The second angel then follows with the announcement of Babylon's fall. And finally the third message warns everyone not to accept the erroneous teachings coming out of Babylon.

Because the second angel's message announcing the fall of Babylon follows the historic events tied to the first angel's message, Babylon's fall is a result of rejecting the advent message of Miller and the evidence of the seventh-day Sabbath. The book, *The Great Controversy*, orders the progressive events in Babylon's fall as follows:

1. The second angel's message was first preached in the summer of 1844 and was accompanied by a marked declension in the spiritual life of nearly all the churches when they rejected the message of the second advent.[1]

2. Because the second angel's message was first preached in the summer of 1844, this message cannot refer to the Roman Catholic Church alone because Rome has been in a fallen condition for centuries.[2]

3. The second angel's message applies primarily to the experience of the Protestant churches which at one time began a reform within Christianity and started a movement away from the errors of Rome. However, by refusing to accept the next step in reformation (the preadvent judgment in heaven), these churches began a spiritual fall. But at the time of the writing of *The Great Controversy*, this fall was not yet compete.[3]

4. The fall will be complete, however, when Protestantism, 1) accepts the masterful deceptions and lies of Satan at the end of time, and 2) the union *"with the world shall be fully accomplished throughout Christendom."*[4]

We are very close to that point now. The warning of the second angel will be given again with the appeal by Jesus to His people who are still in Babylon to come out of her so they will not be involved in her destruction (Rev. 18:1-4).

Third angel's message. The third part of the ideological counteroffensive by Jesus is a warning that cannot be misunderstood. The full force of this warning will be see when the fall of Babylon is complete. The message is, if anyone gives obedience to the sea beast and to the image to the sea beast, and if anyone receives the mark of the sea beast, he will be destroyed in the fire that cleanses the earth of sin and all reminders of sin (Rev. 14:9-11). This warning counters Satan's threat that if anyone does not worship the image of the beast he will be under a death decree. Every human that goes through the fourth battle will be faced with two choices, 1) remain loyal to Jesus and face the threat of death at the hands of Satan's earthly representatives, or 2) join sides with the sea beast and its image and suffer eternal death when God cleanses the earth by fire.

This counter-offensive is carried on by Jesus' remnant people who are introduced in Rev. 12:17 and referred to again in Rev. 14:12. Compelled by the power of the latter rain, they clearly, without fear, lay out the issues involved in battle four. Under the threat of death and under an economic ban they hasten from place to place presenting the Sabbath of the Creator more fully.[5] The Scriptural evidence that is presented is unanswerable, and filled with the Holy Spirit they are unstoppable. And Satan is angry.

Ellen White says, *"The Sabbath will be the great test of loyalty; for it is the point of truth especially controverted. When the final test shall be brought upon men, then the line of distinction will be drawn between those who serve God and those who serve Him not."*[6]

Climax Of Jesus' Ideological Counter-Offensive

With the ideological war in battle four clearly outlined in Rev. 13 and 14, we now come to its climax. Jesus descends from heaven on a cloud with a sharp sickle in His hand to reap the harvest of the earth (Rev. 14:14-16). There are two verbal pictures of Jesus' return in Revelation. The one we have in Rev. 14 and the appearance of Jesus as a Warrior-King in Rev. 19. The description of Jesus' return in Chapter 19 is the climax of His counter-offensive against Satan's firefights, and thus He is pictured as a conquering Warrior. The description of Jesus' return in Rev. 14 is the climax of His counter-offensive against Satan's ideological war.

In Rev. 14, the preaching of the three angels' messages sows the earth with truth and counteracts Satan's lies. Therefore when Jesus returns, He comes on the clouds of heaven to reap the harvest that this truth has produced. But Rev. 14 also presents a second reaping. An angel with a sharp sickle reaps clusters of grapes. These grapes represent those who have rejected the warnings of the three angels and are now fully ripe for destruction. They are gathered together and thrown into the great winepress of God's wrath (Rev. 14:17-20).

Thus we see Jesus' response to the first phase of Satan's military strategy in battle four and its victorious climax. Jesus now reveals to John how He will respond to the second phase in battle four—the firefights.

Reference

1. White, *The Great Controversy*, pp. 376, 389.

2. Ibid., p. 383.

3. Ibid., p. 389.

4. Ibid., p. 390.

5. White, Ellen G. *Early Writings*, Washington, D.C., Review and Herald Publishing Association, 1945, p. 85.

6. _____, *The Great Controversy*, p. 605.

Chapter Six

Jesus' Counter-Offensive: Firefights

As we begin this chapter, let's draw an illustration from current events. America is fighting a terrible and difficult war against terrorism. It is difficult because the enemy is invisible. They are dressed in civilian clothing, freely walk the streets, and drive through traffic. When videos of executions are released, the enemy wear hoods so they cannot be identified. The war is terrible because so many people have died. Our troops are attacked by terrorists who appear as ordinary civilians. Innocent civilians are murdered to advance the cause of the terrorists. What is happening in the Middle East is an outgrowth of the great controversy and demonstrates the hatred and anger of Satan. It is clear that we cannot back down or things will only get worse. Therefore America and those allies who will support us must take the fight to the enemy. If we don't, the loss of innocent life will be far greater than it is now.

In Revelation 15 and 16, Jesus takes the firefight in battle four of the great controversy to the enemy. We have seen how Jesus will bring the ideological conflict in battle four to a victorious conclusion, now He directs John's attention to the second phase of the battle—the firefights. This phase of Jesus' counter-offensive begins with the introduction to the seven last plagues. In Rev. 15, John is shown the seven angels who receive the seven bowls filled with the wrath of God (v. 1, 7).

Between the introduction of these seven angels in verse one and the preparation that takes place in heaven for the pouring out of the plagues there is an interlude in vv. 2-4. In this interlude a victorious group of people are pictured as standing on a sea of glass and having the harps of God (v. 2). They are said to have gotten the victory over the beast, his image, the mark of the beast, and the number of his name. Having gained this victory through the blood of the Lamb, they now stand glorified before God. This group is none other than the 144,000 who have survived the masterful deceptions of Satan in the ideological conflict and the firefights of battle four. They were presented in Rev. 14:1-5 as the answer to the arrogant question asked by those who chose to worship the sea beast, *"Who is able to make war with him?"* (Rev. 13:4).

Thus Revelation pictures the 144,000 as surviving, (1) the total destruction of the earth when the Father and the Lamb return to gather the faithful (Rev. 6:14-17), (2) Satan's attempt to annihilate the remnant (Rev. 13:11-18), and (3) the seven last plagues (Rev. 16). That is why when they sing of their experience all others remain silent and listen. No one can join them in singing their song for no other beings in God's vast universe have experienced what they have gone through (Rev. 14:3).

Whereas the 144,000 are presented as survivors *after* the description of the return of the Father and the Lamb and *after* Satan's firefights in the death decree and the economic ban, they are presented as survivors of the plagues *before* the plagues are described. Concerning these plagues John says, *"for in them the wrath of God is complete"* (Rev. 16:1). Mercy no longer protects those who have turned away from the saving grace of Jesus and now plot the death of His remnant. The plagues are so devastating, the survivors are presented to the reader before the question can be asked, *"Who can live through this experience?"*

As the seven angels receive the golden bowls filled with the wrath of God, the temple in heaven is filled with the blinding glory of God and no one is able to enter it until the plagues have been poured out (Rev. 16:8). Jesus' work as man's Mediator is over. The High Priest no longer ministers at the alter of mercy. Probation is closed and the temple is inaccessible . Everyone's decision has been made as to where they stand in the great controversy. It is now time for Jesus' firefight, the second phase of His counter-offensive in battle four.

Concerning the seven last plagues, Ellen White says, *"These plagues are not universal, or the inhabitants of the earth would be wholly cut off. Yet they will be the most awful scourges that have ever been known to mortals. All the judgments upon men, prior to the close of probation, have been mingled with mercy. The pleading blood of Christ has shielded the sinner from receiving the full measure of his guilt; but in the final judgment, wrath is poured out unmixed with mercy."*[1]

The Plagues

The plagues appear in rapid succession throughout the world. Loathsome sores upon those who have the mark of the beast and worship its image (Rev. 16:2), bodies of salt water turned into the blood of a dead man (v. 3), fresh water turned into blood (v. 4), a scorching sun (v. 8), and absolute darkness (v. 10). While humans and nature suffer under these five plagues, the sixth plague pictures a desperate world preparing for the final assault upon the remnant for they are being blamed as the cause of the plagues. This assault is popularly know as the Battle of Armageddon.

As the sixth angel pours out his bowl of wrath several things happen. First, the river Euphrates is dried up to prepare the way for the kings of the east (v. 12). For decades it has been thought that this would lead to a literal military conflict between the west and the east—the last battle between the nations of earth. However, as a part of Jesus' firefight, Armageddon is a clash between two supernatural powers. The drying up of the Euphrates has also been thought to represent the drying up of the popular support for the sea beast and modern spiritual Babylon which is described in Rev. 13. However, the prophecy clearly states that while the Euphrates is drying up spiritual Babylon is being used by Satan to rally the world to his final assault on God's people. So spiritual Babylon has not, as yet, lost its popular support.

Second, whatever is represented by the drying of the Euphrates, this much we know. It is directly connected with the preparation for the appearance of the Kings of the east, and, third, it is connected with the coalition described in vv. 13, 14.

The Kings of the east that will be engaged in the battle of Armageddon will oppose the coalition of nations that Satan will put together to fight the last engagement in battle four. The east is the direction of the compass that focuses our attention on God's throne. The wise men at the time of Jesus' birth saw a star in the east (Mt. 2:9) which then led them west to Bethlehem. The angel who has the seal of God approaches earth from the east to do his work of sealing (Rev. 7:2). The constellation Orion is always seen in the east, and it is from this constellation that the voice of God is heard delivering His people from the annihilation planned by the coalition of Rev. 16:13, 14, and the holy city, New Jerusalem, descends to Planet Earth from Orion.[2] The Kings of the east are the Father and the Lamb who are presented in the sixth seal as coming to get their people (Rev. 6:14-17).

Coalition of Evil

The sixth plague describes Satan's plans to bring the whole world under his control for the last engagement of battle four. This is the preparation for the *"battle of the great day of God Almighty"* (Rev. 16:14). The battle itself, however, is fought under the seventh plague, it is interrupted by the millennium, and then concluded after the millennium when Satan leads the great multitude of the lost against the Holy City, the New Jerusalem (Rev. 20:7-9). Preparations for the final engagement are made through a coalition of three religious powers—the dragon (spiritualism in all its forms), the sea beast, and the false prophet (vv. 13). Some have wondered who the false prophet is. Its identity is made clear in Rev. 19:20 where the false prophet is presented as the power that *"worked signs in the presence of the sea beast and deceived those who received the mark of the beast and who worshiped his image."* This verse is a summary of Rev. 13:11-18 which introduces the development of a church-state relationship, *i.e.* the image to the sea beast, in the United States.

The development of this threefold union between the dragon (spiritualism), the sea beast (Rome), and the false prophet (Protestantism) is described by Ellen White. It is interesting to note that Protestants will be the moving force in bring this coalition together.

"Through the two great errors, the immortality of the soul and Sunday sacredness, Satan will bring the people under his deceptions. While the former lays the foundation of Spiritualism, the latter creates a bond of sympathy with Rome. The Protestants of the United States will be foremost in stretching their hands across the gulf to grasp the hand of Spiritualism. They will reach over the abyss to clasp hands with the Roman power; and under the influence of this threefold union, this country will follow in the steps of Rome in trampling on the rights of conscience."[3]

John tells us that the cooperation between this unholy alliance will become the channel for masterful deceptions. *For unclean spirits like frogs, which are the spirits of demons, come out of the mouths of this unholy trinity, and they deceive the kings of the earth and gather them together for the battle of the great day of God Almighty* (Rev. 16:13, 14). Spiritualism and supernatural manifestations will be the driving force that will bring the political and religious worlds together to carry out Satan's purposes.

The events under the sixth plague take place after the close of probation. But Satan also uses supernatural manifestations to deceive the world and lead it to reject the three angels' messages just before the close of probation. He will use spiritualism as a weapon during the ideological phase of battle four to gain support for the national Sunday law.

"Communications from the spirits will declare that God has sent them to convince the rejecters of Sunday of their error, affirming that the laws of the land should be obeyed as the law of God. They will lament the great wickedness in the world, and second the testimony of religious teachers, that the degraded state of morals is caused by the desecrations of Sunday."[4]

"The apostles, as personated by these lying spirits, are made to contradict what they wrote at the dictation of the Holy Spirit when on earth. They deny the divine origin of the Bible, and thus tear away the foundation of the Christian's hope, and put out the light that reveals the way to heaven....And to take the place of the word of God he [Satan] holds out spiritual manifestations.[5]

These deceptions are set up by Satan to bring Christians under his control. But he also has deceptions for the non-Christian world, *"As we near the close of time, there will be greater and still greater external parade of heathen power; heathen deities will manifest their sig-*

nal power, and will exhibit themselves before the cities of the world."[6]

It is clear by now that spiritualism will be Satan's weapon of choice to deceive the world into worshiping the beast, the image of the beast, and to receive the mark of the beast. It is his plan to sweep the whole world under the banner of spiritualism.

"The line of distinction between professed Christians and the ungodly is now hardly distinguishable. Church members love what the world loves, and are ready to join with them; Satan determines to unite them in one body, and thus strengthen his cause by sweeping all into the ranks of Spiritualism."[7]

Spiritualism is commonly thought of as appearances of the dead. But much more comes under its umbrella. Here is a definition of spiritualism given by Ellen White, *"Spiritualism teaches 'that man is the creature of progression; that it is his destiny from his birth to progress, even to eternity, towards the Godhead.'"*[8] Certainly eastern mysticism and transcendental meditation as taught by Hinduism and Buddhism fall into this category as well as the teachings of the New Age Movement. But have you ever thought of the theory of evolution as being identified as one form of spiritualism?

Let's return again to what Roger Morneau learned from the spirit priest as he prepared for indoctrination into the satanic cult. The priest told Roger and the other participants,

"'Satan's plan to destroy the Bible without actually getting rid of it has to be the most clever thing I have ever heard of,' he laughed. 'Charles Darwin, born in 1809, and Thomas Henry Huxley, born in 1825, both came under the influence of spirits at an early age because medical doctors used hypnotism as a form of anesthetic.

"'The spirits decided that when the two children became adults, they would be the instruments to advance the religion that we know as the theory of evolution. By tying it in with the scientific revolution

breaking across the world most people would never even recognize it was a religion-a religion that crossed all denominational boundaries and even caught up the nonreligious.'"[9]

Then Roger reveals his amazement at what the priest was saying when he learned something else, *"To my shock and amazement, the priest then claimed that 'the spirits consider anyone who teaches the theory of evolution to be a minister of that great religious system, and the individual will receive a special unction from Satan himself.'"*[10]

David Hunt begins his fascinating book, *Occult Invasion*, with a chapter entitled, "Evolution and Its Role." It is interesting to see someone who is not a Seventh-day Adventist give the same definition for spiritualism as Ellen White. In the first paragraph of the opening chapter on the topic of the occult, Hunt says:

"Far from being a scientific theory of recent origin, evolution was an established religious belief at the heart of occultism and mysticism thousands of years before the Greeks gave it 'scientific' status. And the central core of the ancient mystical theory of evolution is the lie of the serpent to Eve in the Garden, the belief that we are evolving ever upward to godhood."[11]

Satan's plan to sweep the whole world into spiritualism has been more successful than we first realized. According to Morneau's account of what the spirit priest said, evolution is not a science, it is a religion. And Hunt points out that it was a religious belief long before the Greeks clothed it in a scientific garb. All world religions seek the answer to four nagging questions about man, 1) who are we, 2) where did we come from, 3) why are we here, 4) where are we going? The proponents of evolution say they alone have the answer to these questions. Thus making evolution a superior religious system to all other world religions, including Christianity.

As the world is swept up into the ranks of spiritualism and the evil coalition functions as a pawn in Satan's hands, the final engagement of battle four is begun. The seventh angel pours out his bowl of God's wrath into the air and Jesus launches the first steps in the climax to His counter-offensive. There is a great earthquake (as described in the sixth seal), the great spiritual city Babylon falls into three parts (the coalition formed during the sixth plague is crushed), and a great hail falls upon men (Rev. 16:17-21). This is the beginning of the battle of Armageddon, and together with the other plagues we have Jesus' counter-offensive against the second phase of Satan's military strategy in battle four. Jesus takes the fight to the enemy.

The description of the battle of Armageddon now focuses upon the destruction of spiritual Babylon. The climatic events of Armageddon, however, are given to us in Rev. 20. As we go through Rev. 17-20, we must keep in mind Jesus is still showing John His counter-offensive in phase two of battle four.

References

1. White, *The Great Controversy*, p. 628-29.

2. _____, *Early Writings*, p. 41.

3. _____, *The Great Controversy*, p. 588.

4. Ibid., p. 591.

5. Ibid., p. 557.

6. White, Ellen G. *Evangelism*, Washington, DC, Review and Herald Publishing Association, 1946, p. 705.

7. _____, *The Great Controversy*, p. 588.

8. Ibid., p. 554.

9. Morneau, p. 46.

10. Ibid., p. 47.

11. Hunt, David. *Occult Invasion*, Eugene, OR, Harvest House Publishers, 1998, p. 19.

Chapter Seven

Armageddon: The Destruction Of Babylon

I had been in a new district of churches only a few weeks when I visited a brother who was terminally ill. As we talked together, he said, "I am not afraid to die." He knew his Savior and understood that death was a quiet period of waiting for Jesus' return in which the passage of time would seem like a split second on resurrection morning. With excitement and great anticipation he looked forward to that moment. Eternal life, eternal youth, perfect health, eternal fellowship with the redeemed, and the joy of talking with Jesus face to face were very real to him. This is what awaits the remnant as they pass through the closing events of battle four.

We are almost to the end of the conflict between good and evil in our study of Revelation. If you are reading Revelation for the first time, you have now discovered that it is not a difficult book to understand provided you keep three points in mind: 1) Chapter 12 is the center of the book as it introduces the great controversy between Christ and Satan, and, as you are no doubt aware by now, this is what Revelation is all about. 2) The three prophecies before Chapter 12 are a quick presentation of the experience of the Christian Church from John's day to the final eradication of sin. In these three prophecies we see the two military tactics used in the controversy: a) the ideological conflict between truth and error, and b) the firefights—persecution and bloodshed. Then, 3) the prophecies following Chapter 12 are a detailed unfolding of the military strategies and counter-strategies in battle four.

Under the seventh plague, the spiritual city of Babylon which represents the coalition put together by Satan during the sixth plague (Rev. 16:13, 14) is crushed. This coalition becomes the channel through which supernatural manifestations bring the rulers and people of the world into unity to fight against Christ in the person of His remnant people. By Jesus' counter-offensive, as seen in His firefight, the great spiritual city of Babylon crumbles into three parts (Rev. 16:19).

The firefight that destroys spiritual Babylon is commonly known as Armageddon which is fought under the seventh plague. Now in Chapters 17 and 18 the seventh plague is expanded and we are given additional insights into Babylon's fall.

Mother of Harlots

In Rev. 17, a harlot clothed in purple and carrying *"a golden cup full of abominations and the filthiness of her fornication"* is seen riding on the back of a scarlet colored beast with seven heads and ten horns. The woman has a name written on her forehead, *"MYSTERY, BABYLON THE GREAT, THE MOTHER OF HARLOTS AND OF THE ABOMINATIONS OF THE EARTH"* (Rev. 17:4, 5).

The following suggestion given by Maxwell has merit. The scarlet colored beast of Rev. 17 is the same power that is represented by the sea beast in Rev. 13. Only in Rev. 17 the sea beast is divided into its two components, the political and the religious.[1] As we have seen earlier, a woman in prophecy represents a church, i.e., a body of people holding a common belief regarding God. The harlot clothed in purple

74

is a church, a body of people who have accepted error and a belief regarding God that is wrong—the abominations that fill the golden cup in her hand. The heads and horns are the political half of the sea beast.

In Rev. 13, the sea beast with its heads and its horns represent an apostate church and the political powers that Satan used during the 1,260 years to war against the virtuous woman of Rev. 12 in an attempt to exterminate those who did not agree with the dominant church of that time. In Revelation 17, the political powers are separated from the church. This is done so the reader can be given more details as to how spiritual Babylon will fall. The harlot is identified as Babylon. She is known as the mother church (Roman Catholicism) and she has daughters. The Protestant churches that have moved out of Rome and have divided and subdivided still reflect the nature and character of the mother. They cling to many of her errors and set aside God's Ten Commandment Law.

Rev. 17 divides the sea beast of Rev. 13 into separate units. The scarlet beast may very well represent the fiery red dragon presented in Rev. 12 or Satan. For the beast in Rev. 17:8 is described by John as one who "was" (prior to the millennium), who "is not" (his condition during the millennium), and who "ascends out of the bottomless pit" (his condition after the millennium, *cf.* Rev. 20:1-3). Satan is the power that carries, sustains, and manipulates the heads, horns, and woman to accomplish his ends. John says that five of the seven heads represent five powers that Satan has worked through in the past. The sixth head is one through whom he is presently working, and he will work through the seventh one in the future (v. 10). The ten horns that did not have power when John wrote (v. 12) are ten political powers that Satan will enlist in the future in his fight against the remnant. Notice that the ten horns did not have crowns (διαδημα, which is a symbol of political power) when John saw them.

Our main interest in Rev. 17 is the additional detail as to how the woman who is called Babylon the Great comes to her end. The scarlet beast and the ten horns work together to bring about the fall of spiritual Babylon. John says that the horns *"are of one mind, and they give their power and authority to the beast"* (v. 13). Then he makes three very interesting points, (1) the horns and the beast will make war with the Lamb (v. 14), (2) the horns and beast turn upon the harlot and destroy her (v. 16), and (3) God has put it into the hearts of the nations represented by the ten horns to be of one mind and to give their power and authority to the beast in order to fulfill His purpose (v. 17)—the destruction of spiritual Babylon.

Let's pause for a moment to look at these three points. 1. During the sixth plague we saw how Satan will gather the kings of the earth together through the use of spiritualistic manifestations. Through these deceptions he unites the world for the battle of the great day of God Almighty. In Rev. 17:14, John says regarding Satan and the political powers he works through which are represented by the horns, *"These will make war with the Lamb."*

2. The KJV and NKJV say that the horns turn upon the woman and destroy her (v. 16). There is a variant reading in this verse which says, *"The ten horns which you saw and the beast"* turn upon the woman and make her desolate. The older Greek manuscripts read *"the horns and the beast."* The reason why the horns and the beast act in unison is given next.

3. God puts it into the hearts of the ten horns to be of one mind and to give their power to the beast. This union between the horns and the beast fulfills the purpose of God in this phase of battle four, *i.e.*, the destruction and desolation of the harlot. God turns His enemies upon themselves as He did in the days of king Jehoshaphat when a coalition of pagan nations tried to invade Judah (1 Chron. 20:22-24). So at

this point in battle four, God uses His enemies to destroy His enemies while He Himself directly intervenes in their destruction.

The question is, Why do the horns and the beast turn on the woman? With probation closed, with the plagues falling upon the world, and the coalition of spiritualism, Catholicism and Protestantism falling apart, the lost finally see that they have been deceived. *The Great Controversy* presents the following steps leading up to what is described in Rev. 17:16, 17. 1) God speaks in defense of His people, His voice is heard throughout the earth, and this stops the assault of the coalition upon the remnant. 2) There is a terrible awakening among those who have sided with Satan. 3) The wicked are filled with regret because they realize they have lost the war, but there is no remorse that they have been in rebellion against God and His Law. 4) They also realize they have been deceived. 5) They accuse each other as being the reason for their eternal loss. But, 6) their bitterest condemnation falls upon the heads of their spiritual leaders—the ministers and priests within popular Christianity.[3]

Then follows this tragic picture, *"The multitudes are filled with fury. 'We are lost!' they cry, 'and you are the cause of our ruin;' and they turn upon the false shepherds....The swords which were to slay God's people, are now employed to destroy their enemies. Everywhere there is strife and bloodshed."*[4] This gives additional details to the fall of spiritual Babylon.

Babylon Burns

The last verse of Rev. 17 reads as follows, *"And the woman whom you saw is that great city which reigns over the kings of the earth"* (v. 18). Once again we have recapitulation. First, under the seventh plague the spiritual city of Babylon falls into three parts (Rev. 16:19). Next those who are lost turn upon the woman, i.e., the spiritual leaders in Babylon, and destroy her (Rev. 17:16). Then in Rev. 18 we are given another view of Babylon's destruction. The spiritual city of Babylon suffers the vengeance of an angry, offended God. Babylon's judgment comes in one hour (Rev. 18:10,17) and her plagues in one day (Rev. 18:8). The kings of the earth, the merchants of the earth, the owners of ships, and the sailors lament her destruction as they see the smoke of her burning.

Using a combination of desperate, angry human beings and divine judgment, God humbles Babylon in the dust and destroys her. With the destruction of Babylon, a mighty chorus in heaven is heard by John, *"Alleluia! Salvation and glory and honor and power belong to the Lord our God!"* (Rev. 19:1).

Banquet For The Birds

Rev. 19 takes us back to the seventh plague and the fall of Babylon. For John says, *"And I saw the beast, the kings of the earth, and their armies, gathered together to make war against Him who sat on the horse and against His army"* (Rev. 19:19). With the introduction of Jesus upon a white horse accompanied by His army, we have the second verbal description of His return that is found in Revelation (Rev. 19:11-16). The first description has Jesus returning on a cloud with a sharp sickle to reap the harvest of the earth after the earth had been sown with the truths of the three angels' messages. As the ideological war of battle four concludes with Jesus' victorious return, so phase two of battle four, Jesus' counter-offensive as seen in His fire-fight—the seven last plagues, concludes with His glorious return. This time He leads the army of heaven in a calvary charge as the King of kings and Lord of lords, and upon His head are many blue ribbons.

As a result of this counter-offensive, the sea beast along with the false prophet are captured and as religious institutions they are both thrown into the lake of fire (Rev. 19:29). But those who are deceived by the sea beast, his image, and the false prophet are served up as a banquet for the vultures (Rev. 19:17-21). This banquet scene in Rev. 19 disproves the teaching of the secret rapture.

The secret rapture is the popular understanding among Christians today as to how the history of this world will end. All of the details are too numerous to give here, but it is believed that born-again Christians will be secretly snatched from the earth by Jesus and those left behind will suddenly miss them. Luke 17:34-37 is used in partial support for this idea of being taken away secretly. In this chapter Jesus is talking about His return to earth and the signs of His coming. Then He tells His disciples the time will come when two people will be in bed and one will be taken and one left, two women will be grinding and one will be taken and one left. and two men will be working in the field and one will be taken and one left (vv. 34-36). This whole concept intrigued the disciples, and they asked Jesus where these people will be taken. His reply was that they would be taken to where the eagles (αετος, vultures) eat (v. 37). This banquet is vividly described in Rev. 19:17-21. The birds are invited to eat the flesh of kings, captains, mighty men, horses and those who ride them, and of all people free and slave, both small and great. Being eaten by birds and beasts is Old Testament imagery for the total annihilation of God enemies (cf., Jer. 7:33; 15:3; 16:4;19:7; 34:20). So with graphic Old Testament imagery, Revelation presents the end of this phase of Jesus' counter-offensive.

According to Jesus, those who are taken are lost, and those who are left are saved. This is repeated by Jesus in Mt. 24:37-41 using Noah and the antediluvians as an illustration. Those who did not enter the ark were *taken away* by the flood while Noah and his family were left behind, safe in the ark. "*So also,*" Jesus said, "*will the coming of the Son of Man be*" (v. 39).

The Millennium

With the coming of the King of kings and His enemies served up to the vultures, the final engagement of battle four, *i.e.*, Armageddon, is interrupted for a period of 1,000 years. As with the return of Jesus, so there is also a great deal of misunderstanding about the millennium. It is not a time when Jesus' kingdom is establish on earth and there is peace among the nations as is popularly thought.

Knowing there is no secret rapture, review for a moment what happens when Jesus returns to earth. At that moment in time there are four categories of human beings, 1) the righteous dead, 2) the righteous living, 3) the wicked dead, and 4) the wicked living. What happens to these four groups at Jesus' return?

1. The righteous dead are raised, *"For the Lord Himself will descend from heaven with a shout, with the voice of an archangel, and with the trumpet of God. And the dead in Christ will rise first"* (1 Thess. 4:16).

2. The righteous living are caught up, *"Then we who are alive and remain shall be caught up together with them in the clouds to meet the Lord in the air"* (1 Thess. 4:17).

3. The wicked dead remain in their graves unaware of what is happening, *"But the rest of the dead did not live again until the thousand years were finished"* (Rev. 20:5).

4. The wicked living are destroyed. They *"hid themselves in the caves and in the rocks of the mountains, and said to the mountains and rocks, 'Fall on us and hide us from the face of Him who sits on the throne and from the wrath of the Lamb!'"* (Rev. 6:15, 16). Paul also says, *"The Lord Jesus is revealed from heaven with His mighty angels, in flaming fire taking vengeance on those who do not know God, and on those who*

do not obey the gospel of our Lord Jesus Christ" (2 Thess. 1:7, 8).

And so the earth is devoid of human life. It becomes a wasteland, an abyss, the bottomless pit of Rev. 17:8 and 20:1-3. It is described by Jeremiah in the following words, *"I beheld the earth, and indeed it was without form, and void; and the heavens, they had no light. I behold the mountains, and indeed they trembled, and all the hills moved back and forth. I beheld, and indeed there was no man,...And all the cities were broken down at the presence of the Lord, by His fierce anger"* (Jer. 4:23-26).

In the meantime the saved are with their Lord in heaven examining the records of those who are lost (Rev. 20:4). God must be sure that they are convinced that He is just before Armageddon is concluded. Because when Armageddon is brought to a close, sin and sinners will no longer exist. With the records examined, the redeemed satisfied that God is just in His handling of sin, and the millennium concluded, Armageddon and the final firefight in battle four resumes.

The wicked of all ages are resurrected. Satan sees the vast multitude who have chosen him as their leader. He continues his deceptions among them and convinces them that they can take the Holy City, the New Jerusalem, that descended from heaven at the end of the millennium. They prepare for the battle and advance upon the city. Then Jesus launches His final counter-offensive in battle four, *"And fire came down from God out of heaven and devoured them"* (Rev. 20:9).

"The great controversy is ended. Sin and sinners are no more. The entire universe is clean. One pulse of harmony and gladness beats through the vast creation. From Him who created all, flow life and light and gladness, throughout the realms of illimitable space. From the minutest atom to the greatest world, all things animate and inanimate, in their unshadowed beauty and perfect joy, declare that God is

love. "[5]

Following the annihilation of those who have rebelled against God's government and the purification of earth by fire, God recreates the surface of the earth. The end product is more beautiful than the Garden of Eden. As John begins the two chapters that bring his prophecies to a conclusion, he says, *"Now I saw a new heaven and a new earth, for the first heaven and the first earth had passed away. And there was no more sea."* This new earth will be the home of the redeemed throughout eternity. All of the effects of sin are gone—tears, death, sorrow, crying, and pain (Rev. 21:4). Planet Earth will also become the future capital of the universe. When the Holy City, the New Jerusalem, descends to earth, the Father and the Lamb move Their thrones to earth also (Rev. 22:3), and the redeemed will live in the capital of the universe, with the Father and the Son, and serve Them forever.

Never forget the counsel given to God's people that was shared with you at the beginning of the chapter, "The Great Controversy," *"The solemn messages that have been given in their order in the Revelation are to occupy the first place in the minds of God's people."*[6]. *"The Savior foretold that in the latter days false prophets would appear, and draw away disciples after them; and also that those who in this time of peril should stand faithful to the truth that is specified in the book of Revelation would have to meet doctrinal errors so specious that, if it were possible, the very elect would be deceived,"*[7]

And so you have the thematic flow of the great controversy from John's day to the end by the positioning of the prophecies in the Book of Revelation. Now it is up to you, the reader, to plunge into these prophecies and expand your understanding of what they reveal. *"For the time is near"* (Rev. 1:3).

References

1. Maxwell, pp. 474, 475.

2. Ibid., p. 475

3. White, *The Great Controversy*, pp. 654-55.

4. Ibid., p. 565.

5. Ibid., p. 678.

6. _____, *Testimonies For The Church*, vol. 8, Mountain View, CA, Pacific Press Publishing Association, (1928), p. 302.

7. _____, *Manuscript 11*, 1906.

We invite you to view the complete
selection of titles we publish at:

www.LNFBooks.com

or write or email us your praises,
reactions, or thoughts about this
or any other book we publish at:

TEACH Services, Inc.
P.O. Box 954
Ringgold, GA 30736

info@TEACHServices.com